H
GOD
Can and Will
Restore Your
Marriage

A Book for Women
From Someone Who's Been There!

Erin Thiele

RESTORE
MINISTRIES
PRODUCTIONS

How GOD Can and Will
Restore Your Marriage
A Book for Women From Someone Who's Been There

By Erin Thiele

Published by:
Restore Ministries Productions
POB 495
Hartville, MO 65667 U.S.A.

The materials from Restore Ministries are used to stop divorce and to restore families. For more information, visit us at: www.RestoreMinistries.net.

All rights reserved. No part of this book may be reproduced or transmitted in any form or by any means, electronic or mechanical, including photocopying, recording or by any information storage and retrieval system without written permission from the author, except for the inclusion of brief quotations in a review.

Unless otherwise indicated, most Scripture verses are taken from the *New American Standard Bible* (NAS), which is the Bible version my husband, Dan, used and left behind, leading me to marriage restoration!

Scripture quotations marked KJV are taken from the *King James Version* of the Bible. The KJV version is the Bible I held on to, in rebellion by not submitting to my husband's spiritual leadership, since he used NAS.

Copyright © 1997, 2003
by Erin Thiele

First Printing 1997
Second Printing 2002, completely revised
Third Printing 2003, revised

Library of Congress Control Number: 2002090561

ISBN 1-931800-00-6

Printed in the U.S.A by
Morris Publishing
3212 East Highway 30
Kearney, NE 68847
1-800-650-7888

Contents

Chapter

1

My Beloved

"I thank God...as I constantly remember you
in my prayers night and day,
longing to see you,
even as I recall your tears,
so that I may be filled with joy."
2Timothy 1:2-4

Dear Beloved Sister in Christ,

It is not by chance that you are holding this book in your hands; it is by Divine Providence. God has heard your cry for help, as He did mine, and He has come to rescue you. The pages that follow will guide you as He guided me when others said it was completely hopeless.

What He asked me to do was not easy, nor will it be easy for you. But if you want a miracle in your life, it can happen. If you want a testimony to share with others on the faithfulness of God, it will happen. If you really want God to restore a marriage that is hopeless, then read on. God can and will restore your marriage as He did mine.

The Bible says that "the eyes of the Lord move to and fro throughout the earth that He may strongly support those whose heart is completely His." 2Chr. 16:9. He has been looking for you, to help you. Are you ready?

You will need zealous obedience. You must enter "by the narrow gate; and the way is narrow that leads to life, and few are those who find it. For the gate is wide, and the way is broad that leads to destruction, and many are those who enter by it." Matt. 7:14. It is your choice whether to follow His narrow way now or turn back.

This is the time to choose. "I call heaven and earth to witness against you today, that I have set before you life and death, the blessing and the curse. So choose life in order that you may live, you and your descendants, by loving the Lord your God, by obeying His voice, and by holding fast to Him; for this is your life and the length of your days...." Deut. 30:19-20.

If you are still reading and have not thrown this book away, then you have chosen to go on. Tears are in my eyes as I think of the glorious resurrection of your marriage and family that awaits you. I pray blessings upon each and every one of you. I glory that some day we will meet either on this side or the other side of "Heaven" where there are no more tears.

Dear sweet sister in Christ Jesus, God can and will restore your marriage: you have His Word on it. "And Jesus answered and said to them, 'Truly I say to you, if you have faith, and do not doubt, you shall not only do what was done...but even if you say to this mountain, "Be taken up and cast into the sea," it shall happen.' " Matt. 21:21.

Since you are reading this book, I assume that you are in a crisis in your life because of your marriage. Has your husband left you? Have you left or asked your husband to leave? Perhaps you have gotten this book before either of you has taken this drastic step of leaving. Even if divorce has been spoken of during an argument, or divorce papers have been filed, or a divorce has gone through, you must believe that "All things (**can**) work together for good to those who *love* **God** and are called according to *His* **purpose**." Rom. 8:28.

As you go through the personal trials in your troubled marriage, if you really want things to work out for good, you must first love God and really want **His** purpose for your life.

Right now His purpose is for you to draw closer to Him, to let Him transform you more closely into His image. And take courage, for God has said "I will never leave you, nor forsake you." Hebr. 13:5. God has not left your side: "Yea though I walk through the valley of the shadow of death, I will fear no evil, for *Thou art with me.*" Psalm 23:4.

I'm sure that the "valley of the shadow of death" describes how you feel about your situation, but God *has* allowed this for *your* **good**.

Only afterwards will you shine forth as gold. "In this you greatly rejoice, even though for a little while, if necessary, you have been distressed by various trials, that the proof of your faith, being more precious than gold (which is perishable) even though tested by fire, may be found to result in praise, glory and honor." 1Pet. 1:7.

The most important thing for you to do right now is "be still and know that I am God." Ps. 46:10. Then follow God's way. Make sure that everything that you do or say follows the Scriptures; be sure that it follows the Bible consistently.

God has no desire for your marriage to be over. Remember that Jesus Himself said, "a man shall leave his mother and father and cleave to his wife and the two shall become one flesh. Consequently, they are no longer two but one flesh. What God has joined together let no man separate." Matt. 19:5. Also, " 'I hate divorce,' says the Lord God of Israel. 'So take heed to your spirit'...." Mal. 2:16.

Satan is the one who wants your marriage destroyed, not the Lord, not God. Remember that "The thief (the devil) comes to steal, to kill and destroy; I came that (you) might have life, and might have it abundantly." John 10:10. Don't believe the devil's lies but "take **every** thought captive." 2Cor. 10:5.

Don't allow him to steal your husband. Don't allow him to destroy your family, your life, and your children and steal your future. Believe me and believe others who can tell you from experience that divorce will destroy children and steal your children's future as well as your own.

Follow God's way instead. Take Him as your husband as you await restoration, "For your husband is your Maker..." Isa. 54:5. " 'For the mountains may be removed and the hills may shake, But My lovingkindness will not be removed from you, And My covenant of peace will not be shaken,' says the LORD who has compassion on you." Isa. 54:10.

Pore over the Bible, letting Him "wash you with the water of the Word." Eph. 5:26. Pray and believe what Scripture says, not what you see: "Faith is the assurance of things hoped for, the conviction of things **not seen**." Hebr. 11:1. "And without faith it is impossible to please (God)...." Hebr. 11:6.

No one but God knows exactly what you are going through or the answers you need right now. If you pray (simply talk to God) and listen to Him (read His Word, the Bible), He can lead you to the victory that He has for you. Don't choose to follow what others may say, those of the world, friends in the church, pastors, or any counselor who tells you something he has heard or read. If you are praying and reading God's Word, God will speak to you first, in your heart or during your Bible reading; then someone will **confirm** the direction in which **He** is guiding you, which will be consistent with His Word!

Most people, Christian or not, tell you things that sound good and feel good in the flesh. But if it doesn't follow Scripture, **it is wrong!** You will be on sinking sand. "Blessed is the man who does not walk in the counsel of the wicked." Ps. 1:1. When it is of God, it usually sounds crazy (like believing for your marriage when others say "get out"!) and it always needs the help of the Holy Spirit to carry it out.

Don't act impulsively or be quick to move. God usually says "Wait!" Many times during the wait, He changes the situation. God said that He is the "Wonderful and Mighty Counselor." Isa. 9:6. Don't you want the best? Wouldn't you want a counselor who knows the future? One who can actually turn the heart of your husband? There is only One who can show you the right direction. Trust Him and Him alone! There are actually MORE broken marriages in the church than there are in the world, so don't follow any Christian, Christian counselor, or pastor who gives the world's advice instead of God's.

Sadly, too many marriages are destroyed by Christian marriage counselors. They get you and your husband to talk about the past and to say things that should never be said. Cruel statements are lies of the devil or fleshly feelings. Then after the counselor listens to what she has prompted you to say, she'll tell you that your situation is hopeless!

If someone (including your spouse) has told you that your situation is hopeless, then start to praise the Lord. Hopeless situations are exactly where the Lord chooses to show His power! "With men this is impossible but **with God** ALL things are possible!" Matt. 19:26.

Work with God. And don't believe that without your husband's help or cooperation your marriage can't be saved or improved. Our ministry was founded by and for those who are the only partner seeking marriage restoration! All that is needed is your heart and the Lord's strength. "For the eyes of the Lord run to and fro throughout the whole earth that He may support those whose heart is completely His." 2Chr. 16:9.

I have had the privilege of being "counseled" by the Best Counselor and I want to share some of what He has told me through His Word. No two situations are exactly alike; nevertheless, His Word applies to all. "Blessed be the God and Father of our Lord Jesus Christ, the Father of mercies and God of all comfort; who comforts us in all our affliction so that we may be able to comfort those who are in any affliction with the comfort with which we ourselves are comforted by God." 2Cor. 1:3-4.

Search His Word, after you have prayed. "Ask and it shall be given to you; seek and you shall find." Matt. 7:7. "But if any of you lacks wisdom, let him ask of God, who gives to all men generously and without reproach, and it will be given to him. But let him ask in faith without any doubting, for the one who doubts is like the surf of the sea driven and tossed by the wind. For let not that man expect that he will receive anything from the Lord, being a double-minded man, unstable in all his ways." Jas. 1:5.

You must have faith! And where do you get faith? From Him! Ask Him for faith since "All good things come from above." Jas. 1:17.

God's Word, His Principles

Beloved, whether you know the Bible well or you have never even read it before, the Bible ALONE must be your guide to restore your marriage. The book that you are reading consists of all the verses that the Lord used to guide me through the fires of trial to my restoration.

The Lord showed me that I had violated many of the principles of marriage, and He also showed me other sins that I was unaware of or had never dealt with (by repenting of them). All of these sins and violations led to the destruction of my marriage.

It is the same with ALL who find their marriages in shambles or completely destroyed, including you. You will soon find, if you are not aware of it yet, that it is NOT just your husband who violated God's principles. You will find, as I did, that you have done much to contribute to the destruction of your marriage. This understanding will be the turning point as you accept and look at your sins, not your husband's.

The wisdom that I learned from reading and rereading the verses of Scripture that the Lord led me to, helped me to understand what the Bible really was and what I needed it to be in my life – my guide. The Bible is filled with the spiritual laws of His creation. When God created the world, He not only made it with physical laws, like the law of gravity, but He created it with spiritual laws as well.

Just as violating the physical law of gravity will result in the consequences of us stumbling or an object falling, so will violating the principles in Scripture regarding marriage result in your marriage falling.

Another amazing discovery is that the ways of the world are ALWAYS opposite the ways of God and His Word. The way you have been dealing with your husband's leaving you, his adultery, his drinking or drugs or the divorce papers he served you, more than likely is the same way that anyone in the world would have dealt with them. What you will find, as I did, is that this is the exact OPPOSITE of the way that God intended trials to be dealt with in order to bring victory. "...this is the victory that has overcome the world — our faith." 1John 5:4.

When I began to follow God's way, which was the opposite of the way everyone else was doing it, then I started to see my marriage turn around. The ways of the world ALWAYS result in destruction, but the ways of God ALWAYS bring about healing and restoration. "For the one who sows to his own flesh shall from the flesh reap corruption, but the one who sows to the Spirit shall from the Spirit reap eternal life." Gal. 6:8.

I have put together a quick reference in this chapter to help you to IMMEDIATELY get your marriage out of crisis. These principles, if followed to the letter with a sincere and humble heart, will result in an immediate or future restoration of your marriage. It is GUARANTEED, not by me, but by God in His Word.

The more a woman follows these principles, the more restoration she will see as a direct result of her obedience. Those who stay in crisis, or who never see their marriages restored, are those who refuse to believe and obey the spiritual laws of God or erroneously believe that they are above the laws of God. One of the "Be Encouraged" videos is devoted entirely to testimonies of mistakes that kept women from restoration.

If you are one of those who believe strongly that you are not "under the law" and are therefore free to violate God's laws, "may it never be!"

"What then? Shall we sin because we are not under law but under grace? **May it never be!**" Rom. 6:15.

"Do we then nullify the Law through faith? **May it never be!** On the contrary, we establish the Law." Rom. 3:31.

"**May it never be!** How shall we who died to sin still live in it?" Rom. 6:2.

Those who understood the law of gravity learned to rise above it, which resulted in man being able to fly. The Christian who studies the Word of God will rise above the world and astonish the unbeliever who will then seek God. However, a person who believes that he is above the law of gravity, and violates that law by jumping out of a plane without a parachute, will fall to his death. This is why so many Christians live lives full of destruction.

Believe and Obey

If you are like many women who want to restore their marriages, you must not only believe that God can restore your marriage, you must also obey His Word. This book was put together by someone who was desperate – desperate to follow God's Word **no matter what!!!** Are you willing to follow God's Word, no matter what it costs? No matter how much it hurts? The question you must ask yourself is "How important is saving my marriage?"

Receive anything. If you don't obey God with zealous obedience, you should expect nothing from Him because you are double-minded. "For let not that man expect that he will **receive anything** from the Lord, being a double-minded man, unstable in all his ways." Jas. 1:7-8. "I hate those who are double-minded, but I love Thy law." Ps. 119:113.

Faith by my works. If you say you have the faith to trust God for your marriage, then "act" on it. "What *use is it*, my brethren, if a man says he has faith, but he has no works? Can that faith save him?... But someone may well say, 'You have faith, and I have works; show me your faith without the works, and I will show you my faith **by my works**.' " Jas. 2:14, 18. There are so many testimonies of those who chose to "believe" instead of obeying. Every one of them is still "believing" for their marriage, but not ONE is restored!

Tear it out, and throw it from you. Again, how important is your desire to have a restored marriage? Are you desperate enough to do "whatever it takes" to save it? If you don't believe God calls us to that kind of obedience, look at what Jesus said in Matt. 5:29-30. "And if your right eye makes you stumble, **tear it out, and throw it**

from you; for it is better for you that one of the parts of your body perish, than for your whole body to be thrown into hell. And if your right hand makes you stumble, cut it off, and throw it from you; for it is better for you that one of the parts of your body perish, than for your whole body to go into hell."

Through the entire chapter of Matthew 5, Jesus calls us to a higher obedience than what had been written in the Old Testament. Read it to motivate yourself to obey to the point of looking like a fanatic. If what you are doing right now does not seem crazy to others, you need to become more radical in your commitment to your marriage, because that's what it takes!

We all must be like Peter in our obedience. Each time he was asked to do something, like allowing Jesus to wash his feet, he went overboard! He even went overboard when Jesus asked him to get out of the boat. He was the only one who followed Jesus with such a zealous commitment. Even so, Jesus rebuked Peter for his little faith. Are you lukewarm? "So **because you are lukewarm**, and neither hot nor cold, I will spit you out of My mouth." Rev. 3:16.

Trust and believe that God is able and wants to restore and rebuild you, your marriage, and your family. God does not have any other person out there for you, nor does he think you've picked the wrong person. "For the married woman is bound by law to her husband while he is living; but if her husband dies, she is released from the law concerning her husband. So then if she be joined to another man she shall be called an **adulteress**; but if her husband dies, she is free from the law so that she is not an adulteress, though joined to another man." Rom. 7:2.

If you are thinking about remarriage, it is not an option. That second marriage has **less than** a 20% chance of survival. You would have an 8 out of 10 chance of going through another painful divorce! Then it's on to number three and four. Stop now at whatever number you are on. There is a better way!

Instead, "Be strong, and let your heart take courage, all you who hope in the Lord." Ps. 27:14, Ps. 31:24, Isa. 35:4. "O give us help against the adversary, for deliverance by man is in vain. Through God we shall do valiantly, and it is He who will tread down our adversaries." Ps. 60:11, Ps. 108:12. (Please read Chapter 11, "For I Hate Divorce" for more knowledge.)

Don't talk to others about your situation. Talk to God; search His Word for the answer. "Seek and you shall find." Matt. 7:7,

Luke 11:9. "He is the Mighty Counselor." Isa. 9:6. "Do not walk in the counsel of the ungodly." Ps. 1:1. Don't tell others about your situation: "For she who shames him is as rottenness to his bones." Prov. 12:4.

Also, "The heart of her husband safely trusts in her and he will have no lack of gain." Prov. 31:11. And "by your words you will be justified and by your words you will be condemned." Matt. 12:37. "A tale-bearer separates intimate friends." Prov. 16:28, Prov. 17:9. (See Chapter 7, "Kindness on Her Tongue" for more knowledge. Such knowledge is not optional but essential: "For My people perish for a lack of knowledge." Hos. 4:6.)

Ask God for a **female** prayer partner who will believe God with you for your marriage. **Stay away from singles groups!!** You do NOT belong there if you have a desire to restore your marriage! Stay away from "support groups" that are nothing more than "pity parties." If you want a restored marriage, don't attend a divorce recovery group that will encourage you to move on. You have to choose now whether you want hope or closure with your marriage.

Instead of joining a group, we strongly suggest that you pray and ask the Lord for just ONE other woman who will help you. All I had was one other person and the Lord. All you need is one other person and the Lord! You can find an Encouragement Partner who understands what you are going through on our website.

Stop ALL arguing with your husband! This one principle will be a deciding factor as to whether your marriage will be restored. There are so many Scriptures on this topic, pages and pages I could type out for you. Here are just a few: "**Agree** with your adversary *quickly!*" Matt. 5:25 KJV. "A gentle answer turns away wrath, but harsh words stir up anger." Prov. 15:1. "The beginning of strife is like letting out of water, so abandon the quarrel before it breaks out." Prov. 17:14. "Even a fool is considered wise when keeping silent." Prov. 17:28.

"She opens her mouth with wisdom and the law of kindness is on her tongue." Prov. 31:26. "Keeping away from strife is an honor for a man. But any **fool** will quarrel." Prov. 20:3. And, "He who separates himself seeks his own desire, he quarrels against all sound wisdom." Prov. 18:1. Have you been a contentious woman? (See Chapter 6, "A Contentious Woman" and Chapter 8, "Won Without a Word" for more knowledge.)

Remove the hate or hurt; then try to look lovingly into your

husband's eyes. "They looked to Him and were radiant, and their faces shall never be ashamed." Ps. 34:5. "And whoever exalts himself shall be humbled; and whoever humbles himself shall be exalted." Matt. 23:12, Luke 14:11, Luke 18:14. Peter asked how many times he should forgive his brother who sinned against him. "Seven times?" he suggested. But Jesus replied, "I do not say to you, up to seven times, but up to seventy times seven." That's 490 times! (Matt. 18:22) Have you decided to *not* **forgive** your husband for what he has done to you or to your children? The lack of forgiveness is very dangerous to you and the future of your marriage. (For more knowledge read Chapter 9, "A Gentle and Quiet Spirit" under the section "Forgiveness.") If you are having trouble forgiving, get our testimony tape. It is a powerful example of how God "gives you" the forgiveness for your husband as you yield to Him!

You must begin to see your husband as God sees him. Pray for your husband. You need to first forgive him and any who are involved with him (friends, family, coworkers and even the other woman). (Again, see Chapter 9, "A Quiet and Gentle Spirit" under the section "Forgiveness" about the dangers of **not** forgiving.) Then you will be ready to pray for the man God wants your husband to be. Stop looking at the bad things he is doing. Replace that with asking God to show you the good that he is doing and especially the good he has done in the past. (See Chapter 7, "Kindness on Her Tongue" under the section "Respectful" for more knowledge.)

Thank God for these things and take the time to thank your husband when he calls or comes by. If your husband has left you, don't call him! **But** if *you* have left your husband or ordered him out of the house, *you* **must call him** and ask for his forgiveness. This point is critical! The longer you wait the greater the possibility of adultery, if it hasn't occurred already. (Please read our book *Word of Their Testimony*, which provide evidence of how these very principles worked in the lives of women who followed them.)

Once you have repented, then DO NOT keep repenting unless your husband brings it up. This can be counterproductive. Also, whether your husband accepts your apology or not is not the issue. You are doing it out of humility and obedience to God, nothing more.

Speak kindly and lovingly to your husband when you have an opportunity to talk with him. "Pleasant words are as honeycomb, sweet to the soul and healing to the bones." Prov. 16:24. "A joyful heart is good medicine, but a broken spirit dries up the bones."

Prov. 17:22, Prov. 18:14. **You don't have to be joyful about your marriage problems; just be joyful that God has them all under His control.** "All *discipline* for the moment seems not to be joyful, but sorrowful; yet to those who have been trained by it, afterwards it yields the peaceful fruit of righteousness." Hebr. 12:11.

Don't listen to gossip or anyone who tries to give you bad reports about your husband. "Love bears all things, *believes all things*, hopes all things, endures all things. Love never fails." 1Cor. 13:7. Maybe your husband says he's not involved with anyone else, yet you KNOW he is. Nevertheless, you must believe him instead. You're not being stupid or naive; you are expressing unconditional or agape love.

Sometimes it is your family or closest friends who try to persuade you to pursue divorce or tell your husband off for the things he has done or is doing. You must separate yourself from those who attempt to lead you astray from God by feeding your flesh and emotions. "Leave the presence of a fool or you will not discern words of knowledge." Prov. 14:7. "He who goes about as a slanderer reveals secrets, therefore do not associate with a gossip." Prov. 20:19. If you slander your husband, others will slanders your husband too! "Whoever secretly slanders his neighbor, him I will destroy..." Ps. 101:5.

Because you will receive much advice that is contrary to the will and the Word of God, don't share your situation with anyone! Ultimately it will arouse self-pity or anger in you! These emotions are of the flesh and will war against your spirit. God says in Gal. 5:17, "For the flesh sets its desire against the Spirit, and the Spirit against the flesh; for these are in opposition to one another, so that you may not do the things that you please." Listening, discussing or seeking counsel for your situation will also bring in confusion since most Christians do NOT really KNOW the Word of God and even pastors may advise you contrary to God's Word! Unless they have "walked on the same water" they may disregard or minimize God's principles when you desperately need the entire **uncompromised** Word of God to save your marriage!

Do NOT try to find out what your husband is up to. If you do suspect there is someone else, or you KNOW that there is someone else he is involved with, then do what God says: "Let your eyes look directly in front of you. Watch the path of your feet, and all your ways will be established." Prov. 4:25. "Do not be afraid of sudden fear nor the onslaught of the wicked when it comes; for the Lord will be your confidence, and will keep your foot from being caught." Prov. 3:25-26. And again remember, "love" BELIEVES all things." (1Cor. 13:7)

Do NOT confront your husband or the others involved! That is a net that Satan has left. I, like so many other women, fell into this trap. Watch out! You may satisfy your flesh but the consequences will destroy you and any feelings your husband may have for you. Don't talk to the OW over the phone or in person or send her a letter telling her that you forgive her. This is not God. It's the devil playing on your self-righteousness.

So often women erroneously think that they should confront their husbands because they shouldn't get away with it. ALL who have confronted their husbands, out of ignorance as I did or out of ignoring this book or my personal warning, have written to tell me how much they regret it! They ALL have shared that it resulted in MANY horrible consequences! Please don't be like Eve who went ahead and did what she knew she shouldn't!

Once the sin is out in the open it will be flaunted in front of your face, and you will lose the advantage that God has given you as "the wife of his youth." Prov. 5:18. You must remember, "Love **believes** all things...." 1Cor. 13:7.

You must remember at all times that this is a "spiritual" war. As in all wars, it is foolish and dangerous to let the enemy know what you know. No battle in the Bible was ever won by revealing inside information from the Lord! Nor does it tell us to reveal enemy movements. Instead, the Bible warns us to fight this as a spiritual war! 1Tim. 1:18 says to "fight the good fight." "We do not war according to the flesh" (2Cor. 10:3). We are told instead to "Be of sober spirit [which literally means WAKE UP], be on the alert. Your adversary, the devil, prowls about like a roaring lion, seeking someone to devour." 1Pet. 5:8.

Your husband, and others, are working with the devil, as his slaves, to destroy your marriage, future and children. "Do you not know that when you present yourselves to someone as **slaves** for obedience, you are slaves of the one whom you obey, either of *sin resulting in death*, or of obedience resulting in righteousness?" Rom. 6:16. To win this war, YOU must be a slave of righteousness – don't confront him about his sin or what you know!!

Do NOT try to find out where your husband is if he hasn't given you his whereabouts! This is God's protection **for you**! Be quiet; be still. Go into your prayer closet and begin to fight the battle through prayer, on your knees before the Lord. God can change your husband's heart, but you will harden it if you openly reveal mistrust, suspicion and jealousy. "The king's heart is like channels of water in the hand of the LORD; He turns it wherever He wishes." Prov. 21:1. The other woman will then appear to be the one wronged, not you! Every man protects and defends the adulteress when his wife verbally (or physically) attacks the other woman. Be quiet! Listen to the "Be Encouraged" videos to avoid making this fatal mistake.

Don't act hastily in ANY decision. At this time you are not thinking clearly and are most certainly acting on emotion rather than wisdom. "And he who makes haste with his feet errs." Prov. 19:2. "The prudent man considers his steps." Prov. 14:15. "There is a way which seems right to a man, but its end is the way of death." Prov. 16:25 and Prov. 14:12. "Do you see a man hasty in his words? There is more hope for a fool than for him." Prov. 29:20.

"The lot is cast into the lap, but its every decision is from the Lord." Prov. 16:33. "A wise man is cautious and turns away from evil." Prov. 14:16. Don't hurry to make changes like setting up a "visitation schedule." Don't be quick to run to get a divorce. God says "I hate divorce" (Mal. 2:16). Don't move out or leave your home: "She (a harlot) is boisterous and rebellious; her feet do not remain at home." Prov. 7:11. Don't follow her ways!

Have you gone to your husband with your needs, your fears or your problems – only to have *him* let you down or reject you? Memorize these Scriptures: "My **God** shall supply all my needs according to His riches in glory." Phil. 4:19. "I would have despaired unless I had believed that I would see the goodness of the Lord in the land of the living. Wait on the Lord, be of good courage, yes, wait *on the Lord*." Ps. 27:13.

"When a man's ways are pleasing to the Lord, He makes even his enemies to be at peace with him." Prov. 16:7. "Strength and dignity are her clothing and she smiles at the future." Prov. 31:25. Instead of pleading, take this opportunity to thank your husband and praise him for how he has taken care of you in the past. This is God's way; it's called contentment.

Part of your problem may be your career outside the home. Since God said to wait for things, but we move ahead and charge things, you may have "needed to go to work." Now your house **sits empty** while you work, your children are in day care and your husband has his own apartment. Satan is a thief!

Soon you will lose the house that you worked so hard for. Allow God to save your house, your family and your marriage. (See the section "Servant of All" in the lesson "The Ways of Her Household" for more knowledge. This lesson can be found in *A Wise Woman Builds Her House: By a FOOL Who Tore Hers Down with Her Own Hands*.)

Never seek your husband's help and support in your present trials. There is no better way to drive your husband away from you than to tell him all that is wrong at home! The reason he left you was to "flee" trouble. He will NEVER return to a home that is in chaos or come to your rescue – never! A man who leaves or gets involved with another woman is concentrating on finding happiness. If you find help through your "love relationship" with the Lord as you should, when trouble hits (and it will hit!) then your husband will come running back home!

Did you ever encourage your husband to leave? We at Restore Ministries have seen too many wives who have asked their husbands to leave or who have been first to mention the word "divorce" in a time of anger. When you plant bad seeds, don't be surprised if he ends up in adultery. Words have more power than you know. "And I say to you, that every careless word that men shall speak, they shall render account for it in the day of judgment." Matt. 12:36.

If there have been problems like alcohol, drugs or abuse, don't add adultery to them! Maybe you wanted him to leave because of alcohol, drugs, or abuse. Or maybe one of you just felt that you didn't love each other anymore. Please read Chapter 15, "Comfort Those" for more help. If there have been problems like alcohol, drugs or abuse, don't add adultery to them! Men who are out of their homes are considered "single" even though they are **not**! Separation is the first step to divorce. And divorce is a life-changing mistake.

Many older women, ignorant of the destruction of separation, advise young women to tell their husbands to leave or to not allow them to return home. Older women, as stated in Titus 2, should **teach what is good** and encourage younger women to "love their husbands, to love their children...being subject to their own husbands, that the word of God may not be dishonored."

The separation that is spoken of in 1Cor. 7:5 is to be done with mutual agreement AND for the purpose of fasting and prayer. This verse confirms this: "And a woman who has |a believing or| an unbelieving husband, and he consents to live with her, **let her not**

send her husband away." 1Cor. 7:13.

By making a decision to separate or divorce, you will have chosen to destroy not only your life and your husband's life, but also your children's lives and future. Your (future) grandchildren, your parents and all your friends will also feel the devastating effects of this selfish, ignorant and foolish decision.

By suggesting that your husband leaves, you have taken that first step toward divorce. Isn't it time to turn around before things go any further? The world and Satan have convinced you that this separation or divorce will make things better, but that **is a lie!** If that were true, 8 out of 10 people wouldn't get divorced in that second or subsequent marriage. Once again, the Bible is clear: "a woman who has an unbelieving husband, and he consents to live with her, let her **not send her husband away."** 1Cor. 7:13.

If your husband has left you, you must stop pursuing, pushing him or even standing in his way. He will only try harder to get away from you or run to evil. "How blessed is the man who does not walk in the counsel of the wicked, nor stand in the WAY of sinners" Ps. 1:1. The only road block should be a "hedge of thorns." (Hosea 2:6) You should read the book of Hosea in your Bible. We have a prayer written for you to memorize based on the hedge of thorns. (You will find it in Chapter 17, "Stand in the Gap.") Pray it daily *for* your husband.

Many ministries encourage "standers" to continue to pursue the spouse who has left with phone calls, cards, letters and statements about their "marriage covenant." THIS IS NOT SCRIPTURAL and has caused many to become "standers for life"! The Bible says, "...if the unbelieving one leaves, **let him leave**; the brother or the sister is not under bondage in such cases, but God has **called us to peace."** 1Cor. 7:15. If you won't let go, friction will continue. "How blessed is the man who does not walk in the counsel of the wicked, nor **stand in the way of sinners....**" Ps. 1:1 NIV. You must let your husband know that he is free to leave (based on 1Cor. 7:15). This will cause him to stop running, pursuing divorce or jumping into another marriage! (For more information get our Q & A video "Alluring and Unconditional Love.")

But I am already divorced. It's never too late even if a divorce has taken place. Many "remarry" their former spouses AFTER they have divorced. "Don't be overcome with evil, but overcome evil with good." Rom. 12:21. God specifically asked His prophet Hosea to remarry his wife Gomer even after she was blatantly unfaithful to him. "For she is not my wife, and I am not her husband..." "Then she will say, ' I will go back to my first husband, for it was better for me then than now.' " Hosea 2:7. "Then the Lord said to me (Hosea), 'Go again, love a woman who is loved by her husband, yet an adulteress.' " Hosea 3:1. God used the story of Hosea and Gomer to show His commitment to His own bride (the church) and His strong stand on marriage.

Don't allow your children to see your pain or anger toward your husband. Do ALL that you can to shield your children from what is going on. This will only cause them to have bad feelings toward their father. (Please listen to "Be Encouraged" video tape #4 to see how to do this Scripturally.) Don't place the blame on your husband. A wise woman **builds** her house but the foolish will **tear** it down with her own hands." Prov. 14:1. "The Lord turns the heart whichever way **He** wishes." Prov. 21:1. Be careful where you turn your children's hearts. "And he will restore the hearts of the fathers to children and the hearts of the children to their fathers, *lest I come and smite the land with a curse.*" Mal. 4:6. For "The glory of sons is their fathers." Prov. 17:6.

The Lord has allowed these trials in your life, and your children's lives, for a time, in order to draw you all closer to Him, accomplish His work in all of you and then draw you back together again for His glory! When your husband is not around to blame, you can then look to Him! When you are closer to Him, He can change you more into His image! "They looked to Him and were radiant, and their faces shall never be ashamed." Ps. 34:5.

Don't allow your children to speak badly about their father. You must demand respect for their father (whether they are 5, 15 or 25!). "Honor your father and your mother." Exod. 20:12, Deut. 5:16, Mark 7:10. Again remember, "And he will restore the hearts of the fathers to children and the hearts of the children to their fathers, lest I come and smite the land with a curse." Mal. 4:6. (If you have spoken badly about their father, first ask God for forgiveness, next ask your husband's forgiveness and lastly your children's forgiveness.) "He who conceals his transgression will not prosper." Prov. 28:13. Then begin to build him up in the children's (and your) eyes. (See Chapter 7, "Kindness on Her Tongue" under the section "Respectful" for more knowledge.)

Remember, you will have trouble enforcing respect for *their* father if *you* exhibit disrespect for *your* husband.

Don't allow your children to become unruly. "A child who gets his own way brings shame to his mother." Prov. 29:15. Instead of allowing them to vent their anger, use this time to teach them to forgive and pray for their father. When the anger is gone, the pain will be felt; then teach them to rely on God for comfort. This Scripture helped my (then) 5-year-old when he memorized: "For He has said 'I will never leave you nor forsake you.' " Hebr. 13:5. Your children are confused right now, so give them clear directions. (See the lesson, "Your Mother's Teachings" for more knowledge in *A Wise Woman Builds Her House: By a FOOL Who Tore Hers Down with Her Own Hands*.) Again, you will have trouble enforcing this if *you* exhibit a lack of control.

Be careful not to choose the "easiest" road. It may *seem* like the easiest road, but in the end it is the road to even more sadness, trials, difficulties and heartache than you are now experiencing. We, who have gone through difficult marriages, separation and/or divorce, want to warn you against any ideas, books or other people who will sway you to go the way of the world, which **ALWAYS** ends in disaster! If the world endorses it, as Christians we know it is the wide road to destruction.

Narrow is the way that leads to life, and few are those who find it! "Enter by the narrow gate; for the gate is wide, and the way is broad that leads to destruction, and many are those who enter by it. For the gate is small, and the way is narrow that leads to life, and few are those who find it." Matt. 7:13-14. You must look for that narrow way in all your decisions, the way you speak to others, and the way you handle the trials that WILL come your way now and in the future.

Please be careful what you read. The books whose foundation is in philosophy or those written by psychologists or marriage counselors will fill your mind with destructive thoughts. Be careful about reading books that cover such topics as "tough love," "spicing up your marriage," and "codependency." We have seen the damage that these ideas have done to marriages and the women who have looked to them in their desperation.

Look to God and to those of "like mind" to encourage you to believe God for your marriage. Please go to the Counselor (God's Word) which is free and save your money and your marriage. God wants you to Himself! Stay away from the "professionals." Every professional has his/her ways and beliefs. There are thousands of both Christian and secular marriage counselors and books about marriage problems. If they knew all the answers, why is there an epidemic of divorces, especially in the church?!! Choose the Mighty Counselor!

Where do you begin? What should you do? Begin to move your demolished house onto the rock. "Therefore everyone who hears these words of Mine, and acts upon them, may be compared to a wise man, who built his house upon the rock. And the rain descended, and the floods came, and the winds blew, and burst against that house; and yet it did not fall, for it had been founded upon the rock." Matt. 7:25. "The wise woman builds her house, but the foolish tears it down with her own hands." Prov. 14:1. "By wisdom a house is built, and by understanding it is established; and by knowledge the rooms are filled with all precious and pleasant riches." Prov. 24:3.

Praise God in *ALL* things. "Let us continually offer up a **sacrifice** of praise to God, that is, the fruit of lips that give thanks to His name." Hebr. 13:15. "Rejoice in the Lord **always**; again I will say, rejoice!" Phil. 4:4.

Learn to really pray. "And I searched for a man among them who should build up the wall and **stand in the gap** before Me for the land, that I should not destroy it; but I found no one." Ezek. 22:30. Standing in the gap does NOT mean standing in your husband's way!

Take every thought captive. "We are destroying speculations and every lofty thing raised up against the knowledge of God, and we are taking every thought captive to the obedience of Christ." 2Cor. 10:5.

Begin to renew your mind to be like Christ's and to look down at your situation like God does, from above. Get *A Wise Woman Builds Her House: By a FOOL Who Tore Hers Down with Her Own Hands* and work through it with a friend. Get a "Bible Promise Book" from your local Christian bookstore (very inexpensive) and put it in your bathroom. Many women use this as their prayer closet when they have children or a husband in the home. It is a place of refuge and you can pore over His promises to you.

Get 3x5 cards and write down different Bible verses that you can use to renew your mind, to fight in the Spirit (the Sword of the Spirit is the Word of God), or to run to when you experience an attack of fear, doubt or lies. Keep these with you and read them over and over again. Stop talking so much about your problems; listen to God and read His Word. Psalm 1 gives you a promise: "His delight is in the law of the Lord, And in His law he *meditates day and night.* And he will be like a tree firmly planted by streams of water, Which yields its fruit in its season, And its leaf does not wither; And in *whatever he does*, he **prospers**." Practically speaking, if you read and reread this book to the point of wearing it out or take the time to make 3x5 cards with the Scriptures you need, you can't help but meditate on His Word. Almost every woman I have met who has a restored marriage did one or both of these things.

NO marriage is too far gone! "With men this is impossible, but with God all things are possible." Matt. 19:26. Again remember that it is not true that you *and* your husband, together, must seek help to change the marriage. We have seen the good "fruits" of the women who have asked God to change their husbands' hearts, to work on them, and God was faithful. (See "fruits" Matt. 7:16, 20.) "And why do you look at the speck that is in your brother's eye, but do not notice the log that is in your own eye? Or how can you say to your brother, 'Let me take the speck out of your eye,' and behold, the log is in your own eye? You hypocrite, first take the log out of your own eye, and then you will see clearly to take the speck out of your brother's eye." Matt. 7:3, Luke 6:41. We pray the same for you: that you will see clearly how to really help your husband by being a godly woman with a gentle and quiet spirit who smiles at the future.

How long? Many women have asked me "how long" their husband will be gone or "how long" their trial will continue. It may help you if you think about it as a journey. How long it takes often depends on you. As the Lord shows you an area that He is working on, work "with Him." Do not become sidetracked with everyday life. Satan will bring in "the cares of the world" in order to choke the Word out of you. He also will bring situations, emergencies and other crises that will divert your attention away from your destination -- your restored family!

Too often our journey seems to have "stalled." Just take the next step of obedience. Our "Be Encouraged" videos or audio tapes can help. When you become weary with the "wait," do not lose heart. This is the time our Lord is using to stretch our faith and focus our attention on His working in our lives. All that is required is our obedience, which will release spiritual power to work on our behalf. It is not necessary that God give us a detailed explanation of what He is doing. We know that He will work out His purposes through whatever happens even when we have made a mistake. We must believe that He is working with people and situations and arranging circumstances for His good for us.

There Is MORE Help!

We now have a video series that goes into more detail and gives you more help in answering your many questions: the "Be Encouraged" video series (hours of help and encouragement). These videos or audio tapes, I know, will help you. They will answer most, if not all, of the questions you may now have in terms of the practical walking out of the principles that you have just read or will read. It's more about me and what I and others did that brought us victory and restored marriages.

If you are bombarded with others telling you that your situation is hopeless, I would encourage you to order, "*By the Word of Their Testimony.*" This book is filled with testimonies of hopeless marriages that God miraculously restored. If your parents, friends, pastor, or coworkers think you are crazy to try to restore your marriage, then give them a book and watch them begin to encourage you rather than discourage you!

You can order the testimony books, or our "Be Encouraged" video or audio tapes by contacting our ministry at 1.800.397.0800 or at www.RestoreMinistries.net. Most women usually need more than one resource; therefore, we put together packets to help meet your needs and to save you money, based on our most requested and needed resource combinations.

We look forward to the opportunity to help you through our website and to pray for you as you post prayer requests. Until then, let me pray for you now...

"Dear Lord, please guide this special sister during the trouble in her marriage. And her ears shall hear a word behind her saying, this is the way, walk here, when she turns to her right and when she turns to her left. (Isa. 30:21)

"Please reassure her when she sees a thousand fall on her right side and ten thousand at her left; help her to know that if she follows You, it will not happen to her. (Ps. 91:7) Hide her under your protective wings.

"Help her to find the narrow path that will lead her to life, the abundant life you have for her and for her family. Lord, I pray for a testimony when this troubled or broken marriage is healed and restored that you can use for Your glory! We will give You all the honor and the glory, Amen."

Chapter

2

The Potter and the Clay

"...We are the clay,
and Thou our potter;
And all of us are the work of Thy hand."
Isaiah 64:8

When we are going through a marriage crisis it is so easy to focus on what our husbands are doing to us. However, as long as you do this you will struggle and never come to victory. We will learn that our husbands are not the enemy in "Won Without a Word."

Let us learn in this chapter that God many times is not changing our husbands' behavior because God is using the things our husbands are doing as the Potter's wheel and His hands to mold us more into His image. However, if we complain because we would rather He use something or someone else, not our husbands and our marriages as His wheel, we will wander in the desert land for years!

Quarrel with his Maker? " 'Woe to the one who **quarrels with his Maker**' – An earthenware vessel among the vessels of earth! Will the clay say to the potter, 'What are you doing?' Or the thing you are making say, 'He has no hands'?" Isa. 45:9. Let God be God. Instead of complaining about "how" or "whom" He uses to irritate us into finally seeking God to change us – praise Him for His faithfulness! He is determined to bring you forth as a beautiful vessel ready for **His** use.

But you don't understand. Many women tell me as I try to comfort them or encourage them that I "just don't understand!" In many ways I *do* understand, yet they are right that no one except Jesus really understands. "...Shall the potter be considered as equal with the clay, That what is made should say to its maker, '**He has no understanding**'?" Isa. 29:16. Talk to Him about your situation and allow Him to give you peace. He knows what's best for you, so work with Him.

You are in His hand. "'Behold, like the clay in the potter's hand, so are you **in My hand**'..." Jer. 18:6. Isn't it comforting to know that you are in God's Hand? Though your husband may tell you that he doesn't care, or treat you as if he doesn't, your Lord does. Who else do you need? The truth is that your husband does care. My husband, Dan, shares on video #4 the truth about what your husband is *really* thinking and feeling.

God's Prescription

God has a prescription for healing a nation or a family. He says if "My people who are called by My name **humble** themselves and **pray**, and **seek My face** and **turn from their wicked ways**, then I will *hear* from heaven, will *forgive* their sin, and will *heal* their land." 2Chr. 7:14.

God told us that if we would **humble** ourselves, if we pray, if we seek His face (not His hand) AND turn from our wicked ways, He said THEN I WILL: hear, forgive and heal us. Instead, we "walk in the counsel of the wicked" (Ps. 1:1) and "trust in mankind" (Jer. 17:5), so now we suffer the consequences – superficial healing! "The brokenness of His people is healed superficially." Jer. 8:11. "And they have healed the brokenness of My people superficially, saying, 'Peace, peace,' but there is no peace." Jer. 6:14.

Instead we are to die to self. "...and He died for all that they who live should no longer live **for themselves**, but *for Him* who died and rose again on *their behalf*." 2Cor. 5:15.

Only the Humble

Humble yourself. Self-willed, haughty people understand the Word without the Spirit, but to know the mind of God we need **humility**!

Humility will be tested. "...He might **humble** you, **testing** you, to know *what was in your heart*, whether you would *keep His commandments* or not." Deut. 8:2.

Humility will save you. "When you are **cast down**, you will *speak with confidence* and the **humble** person He will **save**." Job 22:29.

Humility will strengthen your heart. "O Lord, Thou hast **heard** the *desire* of the **humble**; Thou wilt **strengthen their heart**, Thou wilt *incline Thine ear....*" Ps. 10:17.

Only the humble will be exalted. "He has brought down rulers from their thrones, And has **exalted** those who were **humble**." Luke 1:52.

Only the humble will be given the grace that they need. "But He gives a greater grace. Therefore it says, 'GOD IS OPPOSED TO THE PROUD, BUT **GIVES GRACE** TO THE **HUMBLE**.' Humble yourselves in the presence of the Lord, and He will exalt you." Jas. 4:6, 10.

Humility is rooted in the spirit. "To sum up, let all be harmonious, sympathetic, brotherly, kindhearted, and **humble** *in spirit....*" 1 Pet. 3:8. Your false humility will be manifested in a self-righteous attitude.

Spiritual Arrogance. Over half of those who come to our ministry for help to restore their marriages exhibit spiritual arrogance or self-righteousness. This is what I refer to as a Pharisee spirit. Ladies, this is so dangerous. It WILL prevent God from moving your marriage toward restoration and it is what is really driving your husband away.

God showed me, in His Word, that Jesus was only harsh, critical, and opposed to one set of individuals – the Pharisees! And I was one of them! There are so many Christian women who pretend to be spiritual on the outside but are filthy on the inside. There are so many women who look at their husband's sins yet neglect to look at the log in their own eye. Ladies, this was me! I saw my husband, and HIS sin of adultery. However, no one could see my contentiousness, my deceitfulness, or my spiritual arrogance.

Others saw me (and I saw myself) as the "poor victim" who had been abandoned and cheated on. But *I,* in my self-righteousness, was willing to forgive. *I was* the one desperately trying to hold our broken family together. *I was* the one waiting, with open arms, to forgive my husband, "the sinner," when he came to his senses, by repenting and coming back home from the far country! Scribe, Pharisee, "whitewashed tomb"!!

If you can identify with this sinful and prideful mindset, if this is you, I would beg you to get on your face before God and ask Him to cleanse you of this attitude that will not only inhibit restoration, but also put you in opposition to a sincere and intimate relationship with God.

Pray! Begin by praying Psalm 51:2-4. "Wash me thoroughly from my iniquity, And cleanse me from my sin. For I know my transgressions, And my sin is ever before me. Against Thee, Thee only, I have sinned, And done what is evil in Thy sight, So that Thou art justified when Thou dost speak, And blameless when Thou dost judge." There is much more on praying is the last two chapters of this book.

Seek My Face. "If...My people who are called by My name humble themselves and pray, and **seek My face**..." 2Chr. 7:13. "Seek the Lord and His strength; **Seek His face** *continually.*" 1Chr. 16:11. "...**seek My face**; In their affliction they will **earnestly** seek Me." Hosea 5:15.

They...were radiant. "They **looked to Him** and were **radiant**, and their faces shall never be ashamed." Ps. 34:5. Seek His face! So many seek His hand (what He can do for "me"). But those who seek the face of God, will inherit all things!

Turn from your wicked ways. "If...My people who are called by My name humble themselves and pray, and seek My face and **turn from their wicked ways**..." 2Chr. 7:13. Scriptures are not only for the head; they are for the heart and the will. To get the real impact of Scripture, we must surrender our lives and our wills to the leading of the Spirit. We must be willing to be made over. We must yield to Him.

To obey is better than sacrifice. "Behold, to **obey is better than sacrifice**, And to heed than the fat of rams. For rebellion is as the sin of divination, And insubordination is as iniquity and idolatry." 1Sam. 15:22. Do you know the right thing to do, yet you do not do it? Obey it! "Therefore, to one who knows the right thing to do, and does not do it, to him it is sin." Jas. 4:17.

Walk in the Spirit

Walk in the Spirit. Being filled with the Holy Spirit will enable you to walk in the Spirit, not in sin or fleshly desires. Ask God to FILL you with His Holy Spirit right now! "And I will put **My Spirit** within you and *cause* you to *walk* in **My statutes**, and you will be careful to **observe My ordinances**." Ezek. 36:27. "But I say, **walk by the Spirit**, and you will not carry out the **desire of the flesh**." Gal. 5:16. **Pray.** "If...My people who are called by My name humble themselves and **pray**..." 2Chr. 7:13-16.

At a Restore Ministries Restore Your Marriage Course, all the women whose husbands were with other women (OW) prayed for their "wombs to be closed." All were closed, except one. God used this child as the tool to mend this family.

We can always trust God to bring about everything for our good if "...we know that God causes all things to work together for good to those who **love God**, to those who are called according to **His purpose.**" Rom. 8:28.

What "Condition" Is Needed to Be Heard?

Conform your desires to His will. Jesus' promise is based on this condition: "If you abide in Me, and My words abide in you, ask whatever you wish, and it shall be done for you." John 15:7. When your heart rests in Jesus alone and *your will* is centered in *His will*, you are truly making Him Lord. And to know His will is to know His Word. It is His will that your marriage be healed. He hates divorce and we are to be reconciled; however, He has conditions.

The condition for every blessing. Each promise given by God has a condition for that blessing. Many will claim a portion of the Scripture, yet omit the conditions or overlook them.

Condition: "Believe on the Lord Jesus...
Promise: and you shall be saved." Acts 16:31.

Condition: "Delight yourself in the Lord...
Promise: And He will give you the desires of your heart." Ps. 37:4.

Condition: "Train up a child in the way he should go,...
Promise: Even when he is old he will not depart from it." Prov. 22:6.

Condition: First, "to those who love God..." And secondly, "...to those who are called according to His purpose."
Promise: "And we know that God causes all things to work together for good...." Rom. 8:28.

Your Tears Are Precious to Him

To whom do we cry? Men seem to hate our tears. Is it because they don't know what to do when a woman cries, or because the female has used tears to manipulate him, so much so that he stands afar? The fact that God is a jealous God and those tears belong to Him could be the reason for our husbands' indifference, at times, to our tears. "Then you will call, and the Lord will answer; **You will cry,** and He will say, '**Here I am.**' " Isa. 58:9. "*Do not cease* to **cry to the Lord** our God for us...." 1Sam. 7:8.

This victory may take longer to be manifested in the flesh: We hope for the things that are **unseen**. It will need our faith in God. Cry to Him ALONE, not your husband! Only God has the power to change your situation!

My tears. "I am **weary with my sighing;** *every* **night** I make my bed swim, I dissolve my couch with my **tears**." Ps. 6:6. "My **tears** have been *my food day and night*, while they say to me all day long." Ps. 42:3. "Put my **tears** in Thy *bottle*; Are they not *in Thy book*?" Ps. 56:8. "Those who sow in **tears** shall reap with joyful shouting." Ps. 126:5. " 'Yet even now,' declares the Lord, 'Return to Me with all your heart, And with fasting, **weeping**, and **mourning**....' " Joel 2:12. To find a greater walk and intimacy with the Lord, visit our website first thing in the morning for our Daily Devotional that is written especially for those in marital crisis.

Tears, crying out, wailing. You must find and write down Scriptures that will help you understand the heartfelt sincerity needed when we cry out to God (especially for our husbands' salvation or for a broken or troubled marriage). As you read through them, mark those that move your heart and memorize them during your prayer time, on your knees, before the Lord. We are told to pray, to cry out to God.

Personal commitment: to allow God to change me. "Based on what I have learned from God's Word, I commit to allowing God to change me through whatever means or through whomever He chooses. I will focus my attention on changing myself rather than my husband or others around me."

Date: _____ Signed:_____

Chapter
3

Have Faith

And Jesus answered them,
"Have faith in God."
Mark 11:22

Do You Have Faith or Fear?

Fear will be one of the greatest attacks that you will need to overcome. Rom. 12:21 tells us, "Do not be overcome by evil, but overcome evil with good." Fear will steal your faith and make you totally vulnerable to the enemy. When you listen to all that others tell you about what your husband is doing or not doing, instead of keeping your eyes on the Lord and His Word, you will fail to focus on Him and you will begin to sink!

And you must speak the "truth" to everyone always about your faith in God's ability and His desire to restore your marriage. Again, read the testimonies of restored marriages; then BELIEVE that yours will be added to theirs!

An example of faith, Peter. Read the account of Peter in Matthew 14 starting in verse 22. Jesus asked Peter to walk on water. If He is asking you to walk on water, are you going to get out of the boat? Watch when Peter cries out to Jesus – it is always followed by the word **immediately**. Immediately, Jesus spoke to them and told them to take courage. Then later when Peter began to sink and he cried out to the Lord, "immediately Jesus stretched out His hand and took hold of him!" Matt. 14:31.

Fear. A question we must ask ourselves is "why did Peter sink?" "But seeing the wind, he became afraid." Matt. 14:30. If you look at your situation and at the battle that is raging before you, you will sink! Peter took his eyes off the Lord and the result was fear! It says "he became afraid." If you take your eyes off the Lord, you will become fearful.

Instead look to Jesus and RISE above your storm. When you are in an airplane in the midst of a storm, it is very bumpy when you are climbing above the clouds. But once the plane is above those black clouds, the flight is smooth, the sun is shining and you can almost see and feel God there! Amazingly, from that vantage point the clouds below are white and soft!

Your testimony. Another very important point is to see what happened to the others who were in the boat. (Did you forget that there were others who didn't get out of the boat?) It says, "And those who were in the boat worshiped Him saying, 'You are certainly God's Son!' " Matt. 14:33. Are you willing to allow God to use you to show His goodness, His loving kindness, His protection, and to draw others to Him? There is a great reward! This is evangelism. Others will come to you when they are having trouble because they have seen your peace despite your circumstances.

Overcome

The wind stopped. "And when they got into the boat, the wind stopped." Matt. 14:32. Your battle will not go on forever. This test was needed to make Peter strong enough to be the "Rock" of which Jesus had spoken. (Matt. 16:18) Satan (and others working for him) will tell you that you will stay in the trial unless you get away, or give in and give up.

God never intended us to remain "In the valley of the shadow of death." In Proverbs 23 it says that we go "*through* the valley of the shadow of death." Satan wants us to think that God wants us to **live there**! He wants to paint a "hopeless" picture! God is our hope, and hope is the faith in His Word that has been sown in our hearts.

Faith

Abraham. A second example is when Abraham was 90 years old and still without the child God had promised him. It says "He hoped against hope." (Rom. 4:18) Isn't that good? Even when all hope was gone, he continued to believe God and take Him at His Word. We *must* do the same.

Act on the faith that you have. "And He said to them, 'Because of the littleness of your faith; for truly I say to you, if you have **faith as**

a mustard seed, you shall say to this mountain, 'Move from here to there,' and it shall move; and *nothing* shall be impossible to you.' " Matt. 17:20.

If you lack faith. If you lack faith, you should ask God. There is a battle, even for our faith. "Fight the good **fight of faith**...." 1Tim. 6:12. And "I have fought the **good fight**, I have finished the course, I have kept the **faith**...." 2Tim. 4:7 "And He (Jesus) could do **no miracle** there except that He laid His hands upon a few sick people and healed them. And He wondered at their **unbelief**." Mark 6:5. When the Lord lays His hands on you and your marriage, will He marvel at YOUR unbelief?

Imitators of faith. We would do well to imitate those in Scripture who exhibited faith (you can find the Hall of Faith in Hebrews chapter 11). We need to act on God's promises. "...but **imitators** of those who through **faith and patience** *inherit the promises*." Heb. 6:12. There are many women who have followed the principles found in this book who have had victory over troubled or even broken marriages. Their testimonies will encourage you in your faith. Believe as the song says, "What He's done for others, He'll do for you!" Read all the incredible testimonies of marriages that God restored on our website at: www.RestoreMinistries.net.

Doubt Destroys

Double-minded or doubting. You must not be double-minded. Your mind must not waver or doubt God. "But let him **ask in faith** *without any doubting*, for the one who doubts is like the surf of the sea driven and tossed by the wind. For let not that man expect that he will receive anything from the Lord, being a double-minded man, *unstable in all his ways*." Jas. 1:6-8. "I **hate** those who are **double-minded**, But I love Thy law." Ps. 119:13.

If you have trouble with double-mindedness, you need to read and meditate on God's Word, which is the only truth! You MUST also separate yourself from ANYONE who continues to tell you something contrary to your desire to restore your marriage. And you must speak the "truth" to everyone always about your faith in God's ability and His desire to restore your marriage.

Faith without works. "But someone may well say, 'You have faith, and I have works; show me your faith without the works, and I will **show you my faith** *by* my works.' " Jas. 2:18. Show others that you have faith by your actions. If you believe that your husband will return home, act like it. Leave his side of the closet empty, his side of the bed empty, his drawers empty and make SURE you wear your wedding ring! "But are you willing to recognize, you *foolish fellow*, that **faith without works is useless?**" Jas. 2:20. If you believe that what you are praying for is going to happen, start treating that person as if they were changed!

Don't get ahead of God. Don't move. Don't buy a house thinking it's for you and your husband when he comes home. Instead, wait on this side of the Jordan – don't enter the Promised Land without your husband! God is a God of "waiting." Urgency is usually from the enemy.

Firm in your faith. Remind yourself of those who overcame and thus received the abundant life God promised. "But resist him, **firm in your faith**, knowing that the **same experiences** of suffering are being accomplished by your brethren who are in the world." 1Pet. 5:9. Read and reread the testimonies on our website and in our book "*By the Word of Their Testimony*" Keep the testimonies of others in the front of your mind. Those who believed God and never gave up now have a restored marriage. Share these testimonies with your family and friends who doubt that your marriage can be saved or that your husband can be changed by God.

How to Increase Your Faith

Faith. Read about different difficult situations in the Bible and identify your situation with theirs. Read how Jesus stilled the waves of the sea, to learn of His great power. (Mark 4:39) Read then how He fed the five thousand with the five barley loaves and two small fish, to know that He can do so much with very little. (John 6:1-15) Read how Jesus cleansed the lepers (Luke 17:11-17), healed the sick, opened the eyes of the blind (John 9:1-41), and forgave the fallen woman (John 8:3-11), so you will never doubt His mercy for you and your situation. Again, read the testimonies of restored marriages, then BELIEVE yours will be added to theirs!

The Word. How can we gain faith, or increase our faith? "So **faith comes from hearing, and hearing by the *Word* of Christ.**" Rom. 10:17. Read His Word and the testimonies of others. Surround yourself with faithful *women* who will believe with you. Those who have stood for God will teach you and hold you up. Many times we find that when you feel like you are almost out of faith, you should give away what little you have left. Call someone you sense needs encouraging and give her the rest of your faith. You will hang up the phone rejoicing because God will fill you **full** of faith. Read 1Kgs. 17:12-15 to remember the widow who gave her last cake to

Elijah and the miracle *she* received!

So many come to us for help and fail to reap a restored marriage because they feel they are unable to sow into anyone else's life as they are struggling to save their own marriage. This is unbiblical and contrary to God's principles. Get yourself an Encouragement Partner and help her restore her marriage. Or start a Restore Your Marriage Course in your home or church if you have leadership abilities. God used me and others powerfully as we ministered to others in our pain and lack – and God blessed our efforts with restored marriages!

Obedience. Don't forget that obedience to God is paramount to victory. Don't forget what Jesus said, "Not everyone who says to Me, 'Lord, Lord,' will enter the kingdom of heaven; but he who does the will of My Father who is in heaven. And then I will declare to them, 'I never knew you; DEPART FROM ME, YOU WHO PRACTICE LAWLESSNESS.' " Matt. 7:21, 23. If you "practice" or keep doing what you now know is contrary to the Biblical principles found in this book – your marriage will NOT be restored!

In God's will. If your heart convicts you that you are not in God's will and that you are not following His principles in this book, then of course you will have no confidence and no faith to receive your request from the Lord. Ask God to "break" you so your will will become His will.

You MUST Wait

Wait. Many times the battle will continue to rage on your behalf. You also must remember that there may be many "battles" that must be fought (and won) in the war against your marriage. Just remember, "When the battle is the Lord's, the victory is ours!"

Just like with all real wars, not all the battles are won by the same side, so do not be discouraged if you have fallen short and made mistakes. We have the comfort of knowing that He hears us immediately, but the response may seem slow.

In the book of Daniel, an angel spoke to him and gave us these insights: "...from the **first day** that you **set your heart** on understanding this and on **humbling yourself** before God, *your words were heard*, and I have come in response to your words. But the prince of Persia was withstanding me for **twenty-one days**." Dan. 10:12-13. It may take some time to win the battles, so do not become weary. "But as for you, brethren, do not grow weary of

doing good." 2Ths. 3:13.

His timing. One thing you must also understand is that God seems to work on ONE thing at a time. We must work *with* Him in His timing. This does not mean we need to **wait to pray;** it only means we need to wait for God to change the situation at the proper time. Thank God that He doesn't dump (through conviction) all my sins on top of me all at once! Just use the time while you wait to pray.

Note: Anger is a deadly heart condition, which shows up in a trial. If you still are irritated by what your husband says, does or does not do, or worse, you become angry, you show a deadly heart condition that must be remedied and healed in order for restoration to take place.

Personal commitment: to allow God to change me. "Based on what I have learned from God's Word, I commit to seeking God and His Word to increase my faith is His ability to restore my marriage. I will fight fear by keeping my eyes on Jesus the Author and Finisher of my faith."

Date: _____ Signed:_____

Chapter

4

Various Trials

*"Consider it all joy, my brethren,
when you encounter various trials,
knowing that the testing of your faith
produces endurance."*
James 1:2-3

What is **God's** purpose for our trials and tribulations? Many Christians have no idea why God allows our sufferings. Without this understanding, is it any wonder why Christians today are so easily defeated? We will see that there are many **benefits** that come from our trials and tests, especially the building of our faith and the endurance needed to finish the course set before us.

The most important thing we need to realize during our trials, tribulations, tests, and temptations is that God **is** in control! It is **His** hand that allows these trials to touch us or not to touch us. When He does allow it, He sends His grace that enables us to endure it.

Permission for adversity. The most comforting thing to know is that Satan cannot touch us without God's permission. "Then the Lord said to Satan, 'Behold, all that he has is in your power, only **do not put forth your hand on him.**' " Job. 1:12. Satan not only needs permission, but he is also given specific instructions on how he can touch us. "Simon, Simon, behold, Satan has demanded permission to sift you like wheat...." Luke 22:31.

Temptations. The temptations that we experience, Scripture tells us, are common to man, yet God does provide a way of escape. "No temptation has overtaken you but that which is **common to man**; and God is faithful, who will not allow you to be tempted beyond what you are able, but with the **temptation** will provide **the way of escape** also, *that you may be able to endure it*." 1Cor. 10:13. He is not going to take you out of the fire until you are willing to walk in it, through it, and endure it!

Temptations are brought on by our own lusts. Lust is simply what WE want. Also God cannot tempt us to do evil, but instead it is our lusts that tempt us to do what we know we shouldn't! "Let no one say when he is being tempted, 'I am being **tempted by God**'; for God cannot be tempted by evil, and He Himself does not tempt anyone. But each one is tempted when he is carried away and **enticed by his own lust**." Jas. 1:13. Women are caught up in their husbands' lusts (adultery, drugs, alcohol or pornography), yet they fail to see their own lusts for food, buying or even their marriages! Lust is lust – a desire for what WE WANT!

We are in His Hand. "For I have taken all this to my heart and explain it that righteous men, wise men and their deeds are **in the hand of God**." Eccl. 9:1. We make the mistake of foolishly trying to get things from others, especially from our husbands, when ALL that we receive will be from the Lord!

"Many seek the ruler's favor, but *justice* for man comes **from the Lord**." Prov. 29:26.

"The horse is prepared for the day of battle, but *victory* **belongs to the Lord**." Prov. 21:30-31.

"The lot is cast into the lap, but its **every** *decision* **is from the Lord**." Prov. 16:33.

"The king's *heart* is like channels of water **in the hand of the Lord**; He turns it wherever He wishes." Prov. 21:1.

Repentance and salvation. "I now rejoice, not that you were made sorrowful, but that you were made sorrowful to the point of repentance; for you were made sorrowful according to the **will of God**, in order that you might not suffer loss in anything through us. For the sorrow that is according to the **will of God** produces a **repentance without regret**, leading to salvation; but the sorrow of the world produces death." 2Cor. 7:9. God allows us to be sorrowful to bring us to repentance. When we try to make our husbands (or others) sorry for what they have done, it will not bring true and genuine repentance, but instead will HARDEN their hearts toward us and God!

We need grace. "And He has said to me, 'My **grace** is sufficient for you, for power is perfected in weakness'. Most gladly, therefore, I will rather boast about my weaknesses, that the power of Christ may dwell in me. Therefore, I am **well content** with **weaknesses**, with **insults**, with **distresses**, with **persecutions**, with **difficulties**, for Christ's sake; for when I am weak, then I am strong." 2Cor. 12: 9-10. You will NEVER see restoration until you exhibit contentment in your trials.

Amazing Grace

How do we get the grace we need to make it through our trials? Through humility.

"God hates the proud but **gives grace** to the **humble**." Jas. 4:6.

"For everyone who exalts himself shall be **humbled**, but he who **humbles** himself shall be exalted." Luke 18:14.

"Blessed are the **humble** for they shall inherit the earth." Matt. 5:5.

"A man's pride will bring him low, but a **humble spirit** will obtain honor." Prov. 29:23.

Boasting about our weaknesses, confessing our faults and being humble will enable the Holy Spirit to dwell in us. Then we will learn contentment no matter what our circumstances. Once we are content, God can give us what we've been seeking – our husbands back!

Learning contentment. We see that we must *learn* contentment by the difficult circumstances that God has allowed. "Not that I speak from want, for I have **learned** to be **content** in whatever circumstances I am. In every circumstance I have **learned the secret** of being filled and going hungry, both of having abundance and suffering need." Phil 4:11.

Learning obedience. Even Jesus learned obedience from His suffering. "Although He was a Son, He *learned* **obedience** from *the things* which He **suffered**." Heb. 5:8.

He will perfect us. "For I am confident of this very thing, that He who **began a good work in you** will **perfect** it until the day of Christ Jesus." Phil 1:6. Once He has begun a good work in you (your husband or loved ones), **He** will complete it. And please don't try to play "junior holy spirit" with your husband!

We are to be a comfort to others. We are not merely to accept God's comfort – we are commanded to give that comfort to others, no matter what their affliction! "The God of all comfort, who comforts us in all our affliction so that we may be able to **comfort** those who are in **any affliction** with the comfort with which we ourselves are comforted by God." 2Cor. 1:3-4.

Our Father's discipline. Many times our suffering is discipline for disobeying God's Law. "My son, do not regard lightly the **discipline** of the Lord, nor faint when you are being reproved by Him; for those whom the Lord loves He **disciplines** and He scourges *every* **son** whom He receives. It is for **discipline** that you **endure**; God deals with you as with sons. He **disciplines** us for our good, that we may **share His holiness**." Heb. 12:5-10. When a trial comes into your day, ask yourself "Is this God disciplining me, or is He testing me to see how I am going to react?"

Discipline is a blessing. We must follow the examples of the prophets of the Bible to help others to endure their adversity. "As an example, brethren, of suffering and patience, take the prophets who spoke in the name of the Lord. Behold, we count those **blessed** who **endured**. You have heard of the **endurance** of Job and have seen the outcome of the Lord's dealings, that the Lord is full of compassion and is merciful." Jas. 5:10.

To receive a blessing. When evil is done to us or insults are cast our way, we must endure them, without returning them, to receive our blessing. We need to remember that insults and evils are brought into our lives to give us an "opportunity" to receive a blessing. 1Pet. 3:9 says "Not returning evil for evil, or insult for insult, but giving a **blessing** instead, for you were called for the very purpose that you may inherit a **blessing**." "But even if you should suffer for the sake of righteousness, you are **blessed**. And do not fear their intimidations and do not be troubled." 1Pet. 3:14. If you continue to respond with an insult or another evil, don't expect to be blessed.

Discipline may be sorrowful. Discipline is never joyful when you are in the midst of it. Yet, those who have been trained by His discipline know the rewards of righteousness – peace and a restored marriage. "All **discipline** for the moment seems not to be joyful, but sorrowful; yet to those who have been **trained** by it, afterwards it yields the peaceful fruit of righteousness." Heb. 12:11.

It begins with Christians. Why must suffering first begin with Christians? Because sinful, disobedient Christians will never draw others to the Lord. Again, it is the "will of God" that we are put though sufferings. We need to *allow* ourselves to suffer (usually at the hands of another, even our own husbands) by entrusting ourselves to God. "For it is time for judgment to **begin** with the household of God; and if it **begins** with us first, what will be the outcome for those who do not obey the gospel of God? Therefore, let those also who **suffer** according to the **will of God** entrust their souls to a faithful Creator in doing what is right." 1Pet. 4:17.

The power of our faith. It is our faith that opens the door to miracles. You need to believe that He is able to restore your marriage, and not doubt, in your heart. "And Jesus answered saying to them, 'Have **faith** in God. Truly I say to you, whoever says to this mountain, be taken up and cast into the sea, and **does not doubt it in his heart**, but **believes** that what he says is going to happen, it shall be granted him. Therefore I say to you, all things for which you pray, they shall be granted unto you.' " Mark 11:22-24.

God in His Word has told us that we *will* **suffer.** "For indeed when we were with you, we kept *telling you in advance* that we were going to *suffer affliction*; and so it came to pass, as you know. For this reason, when I could endure it no longer; I also sent to find out about your *faith*, for fear that the tempter might have tempted you, and our labor should be in vain." 1Thes. 3:4-5. What has happened in your marriage is NOT a sign that it is over. It is what God used to get your attention and is now using to change you. Don't give up! Don't let Satan steal the miracle that God has for you when you have endured and prevailed!

With God. "With men this is impossible, but with God **all things are possible.**" Matt. 19:26. "Looking upon them, Jesus said, 'With men it is impossible, but not with God; for **all things are possible with God.**'" Mark 10:27. Nothing (NOT A THING) is impossible with God. Work *with* God. Don't have *your* plan and expect God to bless it. You must work "*with* **God.**" He is not going to work *with you* and *your plan*.

What you speak. "...let us **hold fast our confession.**" Heb. 4:14. "But sanctify Christ as Lord in your hearts, **always being ready** to make a defense to everyone *who asks you* to give an account of the **hope that is in you,** yet with gentleness and reverence." 1Pet. 3:15. "If it be so our God whom we serve is **able to deliver** us from the furnace of blazing fire; and He will deliver us out of your hand, O king. But **even if He does not**...." Dan. 3:17. We need to speak what God says in His Word, without wavering, with hope on our lips. But wait until you are asked to give an account. You **will** be asked if you are filled with the joy of the Lord in the midst of your adversity! When asked about your hope regarding your marriage, be sure that you answer the other person with reverence, respect and gentleness. Never use Scripture to argue with anyone!

Note: If it is your husband who asks, remember, he will be won "without a word"!

Gird your mind and stay fixed. "Therefore, **gird your minds** for action, keep **sober** in spirit, **fix your hope** completely on the **grace** to be brought to you at the revelation of Jesus Christ." 1Pet. 1:13. Sober means clear thinking. Be clear in your mind about what you really believe to avoid the consequences of doublemindedness.

Be joyful. We are to be joyful in our trials because we know they are producing endurance that will enable us to finish the course set before us. "Consider it all joy, my brethren, when you encounter **various trials**, knowing that the **testing of your faith** produces **endurance**. And let **endurance** have its perfect result, that you may be perfect and complete, lacking nothing. But if any of you lacks wisdom, let him ask of God, who gives it to all men without reproach, and it will be given to him. But let him ask **in faith without any doubting**, for the one who doubts is like the surf of the sea driven and tossed by the wind." Jas. 1:2-6.

Be prepared – your faith WILL be tested! Fears and doubts come into everyone's mind; just don't entertain them! Instead, think only good things. If you doubt, you will have trouble believing and the trials will become harder. And remember, we will have a "variety" of trials, some major and others mere irritations. We need to thank Him for **all** of our trials. This is our sacrifice of praise.

Rejoice. "**Rejoice** in the Lord always; again I say **rejoice**! **Let your forbearing spirit be known to all men**, the Lord is near! Be anxious for nothing, but in everything by prayer and supplication with **thanksgiving** let your requests be made known to God. And the peace of God, which surpasses all comprehension, shall guard your hearts and your minds in Christ Jesus. Finally, brethren, whatever is true, whatever is honorable, whatever is right, whatever is pure, whatever is lovely, whatever is of good report, if there is any excellence or **anything worthy of praise**, let your mind dwell on these things. The things you have learned and received and heard and seen in me, **practice these things**; and the God of peace shall be with you." Phil. 4:6-9.

Clearly most battles are won or lost in the mind. Follow the Lord's advice for peace in the midst of your trials to gain victory over them – PRAISE the Lord in the midst of them! Rejoice for what you

KNOW He is doing. Then think on this, speak of this, listen to only this. Many times close friends call to tell you what your husband is up to. These usually are not "good reports" and most of the time they are not lovely, pure or right – so don't listen!

Faith is NOT seen. So often women write to me because they are looking for signs of improvement in their marriage or in their husband's attitude toward them. You must remember that Scripture is very clear – faith is **unseen**! When others ask you about your situation, answer them with, "Praise the Lord, God is working!"

"Therefore we do not lose heart, but though our outer man is decaying, yet our inner man is being renewed day by day. For our **momentary light affliction** is producing for us a far more eternal weight in glory far beyond comparison, while we look not at the things which are seen, but the things which are **not seen**, for the things which are seen are **temporal**, but the things which are **not seen are eternal**." 2Cor. 4:16-18.

Faith is...*not* seen. When you are experiencing what Paul calls "light affliction," it may still be breaking your heart and VERY painful. Remind yourself of the most important truth: these afflictions are meant to be only **momentary**! And these same afflictions are not only temporary but they are producing something wonderful for you – they are getting you ready for a new and wonderful marriage. Remember, the suffering is temporary but the benefits will last an eternity! "Now **faith** is the assurance of things hoped for, the conviction of things NOT **seen**." Heb. 11:1.

Faith – not by sight. Most people start believing when "they begin to see something happening," but this is not faith! "For we walk by faith, **not by sight**." 2Cor. 5:7.

Looking at our circumstances. When Peter looked at *his* circumstances he sank – and you will too. "And He said 'Come!' And Peter got out of the boat, and walked on the water and came toward Jesus. But **seeing the wind**, he became frightened, and beginning to sink, he cried out, saying, 'Lord save me'! And immediately Jesus stretched out His hand and took hold of him, and said to him, 'O you of little faith, why did you doubt?' " Matt. 14:29.

For our testing. Probably the most important lesson in our stand for our families and our marriages is being able to pass our test – the test of our faith in His Word and not being swayed by emotion or false statements made by others. "Consider it all joy, my brethren, when you encounter various trials, knowing that the **testing of your faith** produces endurance. And let **endurance** have its perfect result, that you may be perfect and complete, lacking nothing." Jas. 1:2. When you are perfected and your refining is complete, THEN you will see your husband home!

Tested by fire. "In this you greatly rejoice, even though for a little while, if necessary you have been distressed by various trials, that the proof of your faith, being more precious than gold which is perishable, even though **tested by fire,** may be found to **result in praise** and **glory** and **honor** at the revelation of Jesus Christ." 1Pet. 1:6-7.

So many have failed their test and have continued to walk in the desert as the people of Israel did because they lacked faith. They murmured and complained, which led to rebellion. The proof of your faith, which is a heart full of faith and contentment in your PRESENT circumstances, is more precious than gold.

Keep the faith. Do not turn to another plan when things get tough; do not compromise what you started out to do. Satan is known for bringing new (and wrong) solutions to our trials. Discerning and deciding to stay on the right path is the test we must continue to pass. "I have fought the good fight, I have **finished my course,** I have **kept the faith;** henceforth there is laid up for me a crown of righteousness...." 2Tim 4:7.

If you have been walking with the Lord for some time and have become weary, ask God to send you one other woman who will help you not **bend** from your commitment. "Two are better than one for they have a good return for their labor. For if either of them falls, the one will lift up his companion. But woe to the one who falls when there is not another to lift him up. Furthermore, if two lie down together they keep warm, but how can one be warm alone? And if one can overpower him who is alone, two can resist him. **A cord of three is not easily broken.**" Eccl. 4:9-12. Here are some three-cord examples found in the Scriptures:

Moses, Aaron and Hur: "But Moses' hands were heavy. Then they took a stone and put it under him, and he sat on it; and Aaron and Hur supported his hands, one on one side and one on the other. Thus his hands were steady until the sun set." Ex. 17:12. Also see **Shadrach, Meshach** and **Abed-nego** in the book of Daniel chapter 3. You, just ONE friend and the Lord are a POWERFUL threefold cord!!

A Quick Reference to Trials and Tribulations

God is the One in control, not man and NOT the devil!

1. Justice is from the **Lord**. Prov. 29:26.
2. An answer is from the **Lord**. Prov. 16:1.
3. The heart is turned by the **Lord**. Prov. 21:1.
4. Their deeds are in **God's** hand. Eccl. 9:1.
5. **Thou** (God) has done it. Ps. 44:9-15.
6. **He** (God) raised the storm. Ps. 107:1-32.
7. **He** (God) removed lover and friend. Ps. 88:8,18.

What do our Trials do FOR us?

1. That the power of Christ will dwell in us. 2Cor. 12:9-10.
2. We will learn to be content. Phil. 4:9.
3. We will receive a reward. 2Tim. 4:7,19.
4. We lack nothing. Jas. 1:2-4.
5. He will enable us to comfort others. 2Cor. 3:1-4.
6. He will perfect what He started in us. Phil. 1:6-13.
7. We will have our loved one back. Philemon 1:15.
8. We will receive mercy. Heb. 4:15.
9. We will learn obedience. Heb. 5:7-8.
10. They will produce endurance. Jas. 1:2-4.
11. We will receive the Crown of Life. Jas. 1:12.
12. We will prove our faith. 1Pet. 1:6-7.
13. We will follow in His steps. 1Pet. 2:21.
14. We will share in His sufferings. 1Pet. 3:13.
15. We will be perfected, confirmed, strengthened and established. 1Pet. 5:10.

Ask God for guidance through EVERY trial. "Trust in the Lord with all thine heart; and *lean* **not** unto thine own understanding. In all your ways acknowledge Him and He will direct thy paths." Prov. 3:5-7.

Let us call on **Him** for strength, draw close to **Him** in our time of need. Let us allow **Him** to discipline us, try us, test us. Let us rejoice always in *all* **things**, not just the good but also the troubles that come our way. Let us keep our hope close to our lips and stay steadfast in our minds. Let us always remember that it is **His will** that we face these hard times and that they are for our good!

"Let us rejoice that He considers us worthy to suffer for His name!" Acts 5:41.

"She smiles at the future." Proverbs 31:25.

"And we know that **God** *causes all things to work together* **for good** *to those who* **love God,** *to those who are called according to* **His purpose.** *" Romans 8:28.*

Personal commitment: to consider it all joy when I encounter various trials. "Based on what I have learned from God's Word, I commit to allowing the **testing of my faith** to help produce my **endurance.** And I will let **endurance** have its perfect result, that I may be perfect and complete, lacking nothing."

Date: _____ Signed:_____

For more encouragement and to understand God's benefits and blessings of the trials He has allowed in your life, get Erin's life-changing videotape **Queen Esther: Obedient and Courageous.** *It will help you to tap into your trials that will ultimately set you in a place of royalty and influence "for such a time as this."*

Chapter
5

Your First Love

"But I have this against you,
that you have left your first love."
Revelation 2:4

Have you left your first love? Who is your first love? Was your husband your first love? Was your baby or your children first in your life, above your husband and the Lord? Or has your career been first? Who is really **first** in your life? "He who loves father or mother more than Me is not worthy of Me; and he who loves son or daughter more than Me is not worthy of Me." Matt. 10:37. The Scripture in Revelation says: "But I have this against you, that you have left your **first love.**" Rev. 2:4.

What is our Lord saying to us? He is saying that any time we put someone or something ahead of our love for or our relationship with Him, then we are not worthy of His Love.

Seek first. You are to put Him first in your priorities, first in your day and first in your heart. "But **seek first** His kingdom and His righteousness; and all these things shall be added unto you." Matt. 6:33.

Dirty rags. Ask yourself these questions: Do the things I put first have eternal value? Will what I do today help to increase His kingdom? Am I seeking after His righteousness or trying to muster up my own righteousness? Remember, our righteousness is like **dirty rags!** (Is. 64:6).

What happens when you put someone ahead of the Lord? What does He do to draw you back to Him? If you have put your husband ahead of the Lord, then it was the Lord who has taken your husband from you. "**Thou** hast removed my acquaintances far from me; Thou hast made me an object of loathing to them. Thou has removed lover and friend far from me; My acquaintances are in darkness." Ps. 88:8,18. And don't make marriage restoration first in your life; you *must* make the Lord first in your life!

Does this mean that we are not to care about what our husbands want and need? Are we to have the attitude that "We serve the Lord, not you"? God teaches us a perfect balance in His Word. "Wives, be subject unto your own husbands, **as unto the Lord**." Eph. 5:22. And "Wives, be subject to your own husbands, **as is fitting to the Lord**." Col. 3:18. When we are subject to our husbands, we're doing it **for the Lord**! Even, and especially, if we feel that our husbands don't deserve the honor we show them, we can rest KNOWING we submit graciously to our husbands for the Lord who deserves our submission to Him and to His Word! (See Chapter 6, "Contentious Woman" under the section "Being Subject" for more knowledge.)

Word of God may not be blasphemed. The Lord even gives us a warning that not obeying or not honoring our husbands will dishonor, even blaspheme, the Lord and His Word. "...being subject to their own husbands, that the word of God may not be dishonored." And in the KJV: "...being subject to their own husbands, that the **word of God may not be blasphemed**." Titus 2:5.

Pleasing to the Lord. We are to seek to please the Lord, rather than trying to please our husbands. Then the Lord will cause us to have favor with our husbands. "When a man's ways are **pleasing to the Lord**, He makes even his enemies to be at peace with him." Prov. 16:7. "Charm is deceitful and beauty is vain, but a woman who fears the Lord, she shall be praised." Prov. 31:30. "Delight yourself in the Lord; and He will give you the desires of your heart." Ps. 37:4.

Obedience Rather than Sacrifice

To obey is better than sacrifice. "Behold, to **obey is better than sacrifice**, and to heed than the fat of rams. For rebellion is as the sin of divination, and insubordination is as iniquity and idolatry. Because you have rejected the word of the Lord, He has also rejected you...." 1Sam. 15:22-23. "To do righteousness and justice is desired by the Lord rather than sacrifice." Prov. 21:3.

Your outward appearance. Even if your outward appearance deceives others into thinking you're submissive, God knows your heart! "Do not look at his appearance..., because I have rejected him; for God sees not as man sees, for man looks at the **outward appearance**, but the Lord looks at the heart." 1Sam. 16:7. My husband and everyone else thought I was an extremely submissive wife. Even I was deceived. But God knew that my being abandoned was what I needed. (For more encouragement in this area, listen or watch the Esther video available through our ministry office.)

There is a story of a little boy whose father continued to ask him to "sit down." Finally the little boy did sit down and the father smiled. But the boy quickly exclaimed, "I may be sitting down on the outside, but on the inside – I'm standing up!"

Many times we are standing up on the inside. Many times after you do the right thing and go along with your husband's plan you exclaim, "But I don't agree!" or your attitude tells him that you don't. *Have you done this? Has this been your type of submission to your husband?*

Also you will reap what you have sown. If you were a rebel with your parents before you were married, you are probably still a rebel with your husband. To top it off, you married a rebel. And now your husband has become a greater rebel since you married, just like you have. He now rebels against all sound wisdom and has even taken the rebellion as far as to rebel against his commitment to be faithful to you!

Nothing is impossible. What do you do then? If you believe, then begin to obey NOW! "For the unbelieving husband is sanctified through his wife." 1Cor. 7:14. Yes, it is true. Obey now and watch as the Lord sanctifies your husband. Does this seem strange? Does it seem impossible, because he is so bad? It's because you are one flesh: "Consequently they are no longer two but one flesh." Matt. 19:6. "Neither is woman independent of man, nor is man independent of woman." 1Cor. 11:11.

Can only half a body go one way and the other half go the other? Even if you go separate ways for a while, God will eventually bring you back together. It can happen because "**Nothing is impossible** with God." Luke 1:37. "For He is a rewarder for those who seek Him." Hebr. 11:6.

He who walks blameless. Once you obey, God will turn your husband's heart. "He turns it (the heart) wherever He wishes." Prov. 21:1. Remember, only "**he who walks blameless** will be delivered." Prov. 28:18. If you say you don't want to obey your husband, then he won't obey the One who is over him either! "Christ is the head of EVERY man, and the man is the head of woman, and God is the head of Christ." 1Cor. 11:3. Don't give the excuse that your husband is not a Christian so therefore you don't have to obey him. There is NO Scripture that tells a woman that she does not have to be subject or submissive to a nonbeliever!

And don't excuse your present rebellion by saying that your husband is not around, so how can you obey someone who is not there? You obey what you KNOW you should do and what you should have done when he was still there! If he had asked you to make sure you dress in the morning before he left, or to wash the dishes rather than letting them sit until you have a full sink, then do it. If he asked that you hang the clothes the right way in the closet, stop reading and do it now! If you can't remember, then ask the Lord to bring to mind ALL those things your husband asked you to do when you weren't listening or obeying. Then do them. It is not a matter of your husband seeing those changes, but God seeing that you've changed.

Suffering unjustly. And what if my husband is mean or even cruel? "Be submissive with all respect, not only to those who are good and gentle, but also to those who are unreasonable. For this finds favor, if for the sake of conscience toward God a man bears up under sorrows when **suffering unjustly**. For what credit is there if, when you sin (disobey) and are harshly treated, you endure it with patience? But if when you do what is right, and suffer for it you *patiently* endure it, this finds favor with God." 1Pet. 2:18-20. The Word goes on to say that we women have an example in the Lord and His life. He asks us to follow in His footsteps as we'll see below. (If you are in an abusive situation read Chapter 15, "Comfort Those" and also Chapter 7, "Kindness on Her Tongue" for help.)

"If You Love Me...Obey"

After you put God first in your life, and begin to obey those in authority over you, you must then cast down the false doctrine that says "you are saved by grace, so it's really OKAY to sin, because we are no longer under the Law." Let's search the Scriptures:

Do your deeds deny Him? "They profess to know God, but their **deeds deny Him**, being detestable and disobedient and worthless for any good deed." Titus 1:16.

Do you do what His Word says? "Why do you call Me, Lord, and do not do what I say?" Luke 6:46.

Are we to continue in sin? "What shall we say then? **Are we to continue in sin** that grace might increase? May it never be! How shall we who died to sin still live in it?" "What then? Shall we sin because we are not under law but under grace? May it never be!" Rom. 6:1-2,15.

Faith without works is dead. "What use is it, my brethren, if a man says he has faith, but he has no works? Can that faith save him?" "For just as the body without the spirit is dead, so also **faith without works is dead**." Jas. 2:14,26. Good works are the "fruits" of our salvation. These are the questions we must ask ourselves:

Do my deeds deny that I follow the Lord?

Does grace give me a license to sin?

Am I, as a believer, to produce good works?

I never knew you. Many believe that you can live any way you wish and then enter into heaven once you die. Is this true? "Many will say to Me on that day, 'Lord, Lord, did we not prophesy in Your name, and in Your name cast out demons, and in Your name perform many miracles?' And then I will declare to them, '**I never knew you**; depart from me, you who practice lawlessness.' " Matt. 7:22-23. The answer then is "no!"

Confess your sins. If this is the mind that you had, prior to learning these Scriptures, do as Scripture says: "Therefore, **confess your sins** one to another, and pray for one another, so that you may be healed." Jas. 5:16

Obedience to His Word

"**Wisdom** shouts in the street, she lifts her voice in the square. At the head of the noisy streets she cries out; at the entrance to the gate in the city, she utters her sayings, how long, O naive ones, will you love simplicity. And scoffers delight themselves in scoffing, and fools hate knowledge. **Turn to my reproof**, behold, **I will pour out my spirit on you**; I will make my words known to you.

"Because I called and you refused; I stretched out my hand, and no one paid attention; and you neglected all my counsel, and did not want my reproof; **I will even laugh at your calamity; I will mock when your dread comes**, when your dread comes on like a storm, and your calamity comes on like a whirlwind, when distress and anguish come on you.

"Then they will call on me but I will not answer; they will seek me diligently, but they will not find me, **because they hated knowledge, and did not choose the fear of the Lord**. They would not accept my counsel, they spurned all my reproof. So they shall eat of the fruit of their own way, and be satiated with their own devices. For the waywardness of the naive shall kill them, and the complacency of fools shall destroy them. **But he who listens to me shall live securely, and shall be at ease from the dread of evil**." Prov. 1:20-33. Seek wisdom!

Obedience comes from the *heart*. "...you became obedient from the **heart** to that form of teaching to which you were committed." Rom. 6:17. And again, "for God sees not as man sees, for man looks at the outward appearance, but the Lord looks at the heart." 1Sam 16:7.

Obedience needs *testing*. "Do not be surprised at the fiery trial which comes upon you for your **testing**." 1Pet. 4:12. Obedience *purifies* your soul. "Since you have in obedience to the truth **purified your souls**...." 1Pet. 1:22.

Obedience gives *testimony* **of who your Father is.** "Obey My voice and I will be your God, and you will be My people; and you will walk in all the way in which I command you, that it may be well with you. Yet they did not obey or incline their ear, but walked in their own counsels and in the stubbornness of their evil heart, and went backward and not forward." Jer. 7:23-24.

Your disobedience actually praises the wicked. "Those who forsake the law PRAISE **the wicked**, but those who keep the law strive with them." Prov. 28:4. The prayers of the disobedient go unheard. "He who turns away his ear from listening to the law, even his prayer is an abomination." Prov. 28:9.

Our Example of Obedience Is Jesus

He was obedient *even unto death.* "He humbled Himself by becoming obedient to the point of death, even death on a cross." Phil. 2:5-11. "Although He was a Son, He *learned obedience* from the things which He suffered." Heb. 5:7-10.

He was obedient and submissive to His authority. "My Father, if it is possible, let this cup pass from Me; yet **not as I will**, but Thou wilt. My Father, if this cannot pass away unless I drink it, **Thy will be done**." Matt. 26:39, 42.

Our submission to our authority. "Wives be submissive to your own husbands, as unto the Lord...but as the church is subject to Christ, so also the wives ought to be to their own husbands in **everything**." Eph. 5:22. "For there is no authority except from God, and those which exist are **established by God**." Rom. 13:1.

The secret to success. "All the paths of the Lord are lovingkindness and truth to those *who keep His covenant and His testimonies*. For Thy name's sake, O Lord, pardon my iniquity, for it is great. Who is the man who fears the Lord? He will instruct him in the way he should choose. His soul will abide in prosperity, and his descendants will inherit the land. The **secret of the Lord** is for **those who fear Him**." Ps. 25:10-15.

Self-condemned. Unfortunately most dispute or argue the true meaning of the Scriptures. "But shun foolish controversies and genealogies and strife and disputes about the Law; for they are unprofitable and worthless. Reject a factious man after a first and second warning, knowing that such a man is perverted and is sinning, being **self-condemned**." Titus 3:9-11.

Turn aside to myths. Instead of searching for the truth, many want others to agree with their wrong ideas or decisions: "But wanting to have their ears tickled, they will accumulate for themselves teachers in accordance to their own desires; and will **turn aside to myths**." 2Tim. 4:3-4.

Obedience to His Word. "Do not be as the horse or as the mule which have no understanding, whose trappings include bit and bridle to hold them in check, otherwise they will not come near to you." Ps. 32:9. If you don't obey, He will discipline you. "The Lord has **disciplined me** severely, but He has not given me over to death. I shall not die but live, and tell of the works of the Lord." Ps. 118:18,17.

God is faithful to His Word. "If his sons forsake My law, and do not walk in My judgments, If they violate My statutes, and do not keep My commandments, then I will visit their transgressions with a rod, and their iniquity with stripes." Ps. 89:30-34. If you continue in rebellion to God's Word or your husband's authority, God will continue to punish you.

Read and pray Psalm 51 aloud:

"Wash me thoroughly from my iniquity, and cleanse me from my sin. For I know my transgressions, and my sin is ever before me. Against Thee, Thee only, have I sinned, and done what is evil in Thy sight. Create in me a clean heart, O God, and renew a steadfast spirit within me. Do not take Thy Holy Spirit from me. Restore to me the joy of Thy salvation, and sustain me with a willing spirit. Then I will teach transgressors Thy ways, and sinners will be converted to Thee. The sacrifices of God are a broken spirit; a broken and contrite heart, O God, Thou will not despise."

<h2 style="text-align:center">May God be with you as you
strive to be more like Christ!</h2>

Personal commitment: to put the Lord first in my life. "Based on what I have learned in Scripture, I commit to do everything as unto the Lord. I will show the Lord my commitment to Him and my obedience to His Word by submitting to those who are in authority over me, especially my husband."

Date: _____ Signed:_____

Chapter

6

Contentious Woman

*"A constant dripping
on a day of steady rain
and a contentious woman are alike;
he who would restrain her
restrains the wind
and grasps oil with his right hand."*
Proverbs 27:15-16

Ask Yourself, "Am I a Contentious Woman?"

Maybe that question is difficult to answer because you're not exactly sure what a contentious woman is. If we check the Strong's Concordance, the word contention means: **a contest, a quarrel, strife, a quarrelsome spirit, argumentative.**

Were your conversations with your husband usually a **contest** to see who would win or get their way? Did you win many times? Let me share with you that I was a contentious wife and I won often, or maybe, most of the time – but actually I lost! I lost my husband and the family life we had!

Do you ever quarrel with your husband? "The beginning of strife is like letting out of water, so ***abandon*** the **quarrel** before it breaks out." Prov. 17:14. Yet the world, and so-called experts in marriage, tell us that a good fight is actually good for the marriage. Don't you believe it! Arguing WILL destroy your marriage! And if you continue to argue or strive with your husband you will lose your opportunity to restore your marriage!

Is there strife in your home? "Better is a dry morsel and quietness with it than a house full of feasting and **strife**." Prov. 17:1. Are you the gentle and quiet woman that 1Pet. 3:4 speaks of that is precious in the sight of God? Are your children loud and unruly? Your husband will not come around to see you or the children if he feels strife in your home. Even if you change, but your children remain obnoxious or unruly, your husband will seek peace and solace in the arms and home of another. (For more knowledge, read, "Your Mother's Teachings" in *A Wise Woman Builds Her House: By a FOOL Who Tore Hers Down with Her Own Hands.* Remember: "My people are destroyed for a lack of knowledge." Hosea 4:6.)

Do you have a quarrelsome spirit? "But refuse foolish and ignorant **speculations,** knowing they produce quarrels. And the Lord's bond-servant must not be **quarrelsome** but be kind to all, able to teach, patient when wronged." 2Tim. 2:23. Are you a "know-it-all"? Or do you just have a contrary comment to the things your husband says? God tells us to "Agree with thine adversary quickly while thou art in the way with him, lest at any time thine adversary *deliver thee to the judge.*" Matt. 5:25 KJV. **Watch out for divorce court!**

Are you argumentative? "Urge bondslaves to be subject to their own masters in everything, to be well-pleasing, not **argumentative.**" Titus 2:9. Are you Jesus' bond slave? Has He bought you with a price? Then you owe it to **Him** to be well-pleasing. Now that we've seen what it means to be contentious, God's Word mentions five times how awful a contentious wife is. Let's take a look.

A Contentious Wife

Contentious woman. Have you ever had a dripping faucet that drove you crazy? "And the **contentions** of a **wife** are a *constant dripping.*" Prov. 19:13. Sometimes it takes someone calling attention to that drip (maybe a friend or your father-in-law) for your husband to notice the dripping, but once he has, that's all he'll be able to hear! Have you ever wondered why men move out of their homes, and often in with a harlot? Prov. 21:8 tells us that it's because "It is better to *live* in the **corner of a roof**, than in a house shared with a **contentious woman.**"

Contentious and vexing woman. Again, a man would rather live without water and in the desert heat than live with a wife who challenges him and his authority. "It is better to live in a *desert land*, than with a **contentious and vexing** [annoying or angry] **woman.**" Prov. 21:19. God is so adamant about this verse, He repeats it. Are you listening? "It is better to *live* in the *corner of a roof*, than in a house shared with a **contentious woman.**" Prov. 21:9.

A constant dripping. God compares a constant dripping to a contentious woman eventually causing a person to move out. Why doesn't the man just fix the roof? Because God says that it is impossible! "**A constant dripping** on a day of steady rain and a **contentious woman** are alike; he who would *restrain her* restrains the *wind* and *grasps oil with his right hand.*" Prov. 27:15-16.

Being Subject

A lot of your contentiousness may be rooted in the fact that you believe that marriage is a partnership. This is what I believed and later found out was NOT true! Instead, God has put the family, along with the rest of His creation, in levels of authority. Our husbands are our authority. This is important for you to understand. "But I want you to understand that Christ is the head of every man, and the man is the head of a woman, and God is the head of Christ." 1Cor. 11:3. "But as the church is subject to Christ, so also the wives *ought to be* to their husbands in **everything**." Eph. 5:24.

What is submission or being subject? It is obeying without a word, even if your husband is being disobedient to God's Word. It is not insulting in return for his insults or threatening him. 1Pet 3:9 says "not returning evil for evil, or insult for insult, but giving a blessing instead...." "But giving a blessing instead" means responding to an insult with a compliment and a good attitude "as they observe your chaste and respectful behavior." 1Pet. 3:2.

Is submission applicable today? "Jesus Christ is the same yesterday and today, yes and forever." Heb. 13:8. In Matt. 5:18 Jesus says, "For truly I say to you, until heaven and earth pass away, not the smallest letter or stroke shall pass away from the Law, until all is accomplished."

Christ is the head of every man. How can we be sure that God is over Jesus, and my husband (saved or not) is over me? "But I want you to understand that Christ is the head of EVERY man, and the man is the head of woman, and God is the head of Christ." 1Cor. 11:3.

Respectful behavior. Now that we are sure that God is speaking to all wives, what does He command? "In the same way, you wives, be submissive to your own husbands, so that if any of them are disobedient to the word, they may be won without a word by the behavior of their wives, as they observe your chaste and **respectful behavior**." 1Pet. 3:1-2

Being Subject. "Wives, **be subject** to your own husbands, as unto the Lord. For the husband is the head of the wife, as Christ also is the head of the church, He Himself being the Savior of the body. But as the church is subject to Christ, so also the wives ought to be to their husbands in everything." Eph 5:22-24. This Scripture explains that our relationship with our husbands is to be the same as Christ's with the church. Isn't it sad that many churches don't submit to Christ and His teachings, just as so many women don't submit to their husbands? Any correlation?

Holy women. Where is our hope in submission? "For in former times the **holy women** also, *who hoped in God,* used to adorn themselves, being submissive to their own husbands." 1Pet. 3:5. Our hope and trust is in God, not in our husbands. Therefore, we do not need to fear if they are doing the wrong thing! "Thus Sarah obeyed Abraham, calling him lord, and you have become her children if you do what is right without being frightened by any fear." 1Pet. 3:6.

Protector. When we women protect ourselves because we feel we can "fight our own battles," why would we need husbands? Was it you who told the salesperson off or got rid of that guy at the door, probably with more gusto than your husband would have? Did your husband forget how to stand up for you since you usually took over? Who really wore the pants in the family? Who was really stronger?

If your husband told you something, such as to take it easy or to slow down, did you tell your husband to mind his own business, or worse? But it is a husband's business to protect his wife and children! So what did your husband do when you continued to take charge or take over? First, he backed down because he didn't want another fight; then he moved out of the "constant dripping" house; then he found another woman to give his affections to!

If you remain contentious even after all of this, then when he does come around or call or e-mail he will have a reminder of why he moved out and he will stay out or stay away. This is the reason why so many women do not see their husbands.

You must be a totally transformed and a totally "new woman" the first time God brings your husband around in answer to your prayers. If your husband likes what he sees and hears, he will be back for a second look. This is what leads to restoration! If God turns his heart, but his will overrides it because of your lack of change, then you cannot blame God.

The Root of our Contentiousness...
Self-Esteem!

How did so many women become contentious? We women are contentious because we who are Christians imitate the world and the world's thinking. The books we read, the counselors we seek, classes we attend do not reflect God's Word, which is **pure** and **uncompromising**. Most Christian women are full of psychology.

Poison dipped in chocolate is still poison! My sisters in Christ, psychology is more dangerous when it is dipped in Christianity because we eat it right up! We have been brainwashed into thinking that "self-love" and "self-esteem" are good things, but they are NOTHING more than PRIDE! That was the sin that resulted in Lucifer becoming Satan!!

The contentious, prideful woman, the woman who "knows-it-all," is the woman who argues and wants her own way – because she "thinks" she is right. And when she is wrong, her self-esteem needs to be protected. There is never a humble word or an "I'm sorry I was WRONG!" The contentious woman has been conditioned to think that to make an apology would be too humiliating.

Our pride results in self-righteousness, which is why so many women reveal their husbands' sins, because they can't see their own sinfulness!

How to Rid Yourself of
Contentiousness and Self-Righteousness

If we confess. As we can plainly see, living with a contentious, self-righteous woman is nothing less than a nightmare, not just for our husbands, but also for our children. Let us pray as we ask God's forgiveness. Let us seek His grace to help us become gentle and quiet women who are precious in His sight, as well as in our husbands'. "**If we confess** our sins, He is faithful and righteous to forgive us our sins and to cleanse us from all unrighteousness." 1John 1:9.

Confess. When your husband comes home or comes to visit, ask him for forgiveness for your contentiousness and self-righteousness. If you no longer have contact with your husband, pray for an opportunity to tell him over the phone or in person. (Please, don't call him!) "Therefore, **confess** your sins to one another, and pray for one another, so that you may be healed. The effective prayer of a righteous man can accomplish much." Jas. 5:16.

When confessing, don't go on and on with your "little speech." Just tell him briefly that God has convicted you of being loud and argumentative, which is because you are prideful and self-righteous. Tell him, with the **Lord's** help, that you are praying to change the way that you have been. Give him a kiss and leave the room or say good-bye and hang up! Then, confess to your children and explain to them how God is going to help you to change through humility. So often they see or hear only about their father's sin; it is important that they see that the separation or divorce was far from one-sided.

First be reconciled. If you don't feel "led" to go and get things right, never go back into church. "If therefore you are presenting your offering at the altar, and there remember that your brother has something against you, leave your offering there before the altar, and go your way; **first be reconciled** to your brother, and then come and present your offering." Matt. 5:23-24.

Grace to the humble. Also, be sure you are humble; don't be too proud to come right out and say that you are a contentious woman. "God is opposed to the proud, but gives **grace to the humble**. Humble yourselves, therefore, under the mighty hand of God, that He may exalt you at the proper time." 1Pet. 5:5-6. And keep confessing every time you are contentious to anyone. Once you are tired of the sinful you, and you really cry out to God to change you, you will cease to be one.

Here is God's prescription. "And when they came to Marah, they could not drink the waters of Marah, for they were bitter; therefore it was named Marah." Exodus 15:23. Moses threw a tree into the water, a representation of the cross of Calvary. You must also throw the cross into the sea of your bitterness. Christ died to free you from all sin, including your contentious arguing and prideful, self-absorbed behavior.

Jesus should be our example, always, in all things, in the way He walked on this earth. "Have this attitude (humility) in yourselves which was also in Christ Jesus, who, although He existed in the form of God, did not regard equality with God a thing to be grasped, but *emptied* HimSELF...He *humbled* Himself by becoming obedient to the point of death, even death on a cross." Phil 2:5-9.

Personal commitment: to make others more important than myself, by putting away my contentious and prideful ways. "Based on what I have learned from God's Word, I commit to renew my mind and to be a doer of the Word by being humble and by putting away my contentious ways.

Date: _____ Signed:_____

Chapter

7

Kindness on Her Tongue

*"She opens her mouth with wisdom
and the law of kindness is on her tongue."*
Proverbs 31:26

Everyone watches how a woman speaks to her husband, to her children, and to others. When a woman speaks respectfully and kindly to her husband and children she shows the main characteristic of a "godly woman." However, those who are impatient and disrespectful reveal themselves as weak and immature Christians.

Kind and gentle speech is one of the most important ingredients for a good marriage and well-behaved children. Kindness is the main characteristic of a "godly woman."

We have been deceived by "counselors" and so-called "marriage experts" who tell us that it is a **LACK of communication** that causes marriages to be destroyed. While searching the Scriptures, I found that God has a LOT to say about how much we say, what we say, and how we say it! Follow me as together we discover the **truth**:

It's NOT a "Lack" of Communication!
We Are to Watch HOW MUCH We Say!

Many words. Not only is it not a **lack** of communication that causes problems in marriage, but when there is a lot of talking and discussing, transgression (a violation of God's Word) cannot and will not be avoided! "With **many words** *transgression is unavoidable.*" Prov. 10:19.

Keeps silent. Others tell us to speak our minds and to share what we think, but God says: "A *man of understanding* **keeps silent**." Prov. 11:12. "One who **guards** his mouth *preserves his life*; one who **opens it** *comes to ruin*." Prov. 13:3.

Closes his lips. Actually, God says that we practice wisdom and appear wise when we say NOTHING. "Even a fool, when he **keeps silent**, is *considered wise*. When he **closes his lips** he is *counted as prudent*." Prov. 17:28. "But let your statement be, **'Yes, yes'** or **'No, no'** – *anything beyond* these is *of evil*." Matt. 5:37.

Without a word. God speaks directly to women to remain silent. "In the same way, you wives, be submissive to your own husbands, so that even if any of them are disobedient to the word, they may be won **without a word** by the *behavior of their wives*, as they observe your chaste and respectful behavior." 1Pet. 3:1-2. "Let the *women* keep silent in the *churches*." 1Cor. 14:34.

Gentle and quiet spirit. God finds the quiet woman precious to Him. Is this you? "...with the imperishable quality of a **gentle and quiet spirit,** which is *precious* in the sight of God." 1Pet. 3:4. "Guard what has been entrusted to you, avoiding **worldly** and **empty chatter** and the opposing arguments of what is **falsely** called '*knowledge*' – which some have professed and thus *gone astray from the faith*." 1Tim 6:20.

God Tells Us to Be Careful WHAT We Say

Guards his mouth. How many times have you gotten into trouble through the words you have spoken? "The mouth of the righteous flows with wisdom, but the **perverted tongue** will be *cut out*." Prov. 10:31. "There is one who **speaks rashly** like *thrusts of a sword,* but the **tongue** of the **wise** *brings healing*." Prov. 12:18. "He who **guards his mouth** and **his tongue** guards his soul *from trouble*." Prov. 21:23.

What proceeds out of the mouth. This statement is clear. What you say is VERY important! "For by **your words** you shall be **justified**, and by **your words** you shall be *condemned*." Matt. 12:37. "Not what enters into the mouth that defiles the man, but **what proceeds out of the mouth**, this *defiles the man*." Matt. 15:11. "*...put them all aside*; anger, wrath, malice, **slander** and **abusive speech**...." Col. 3:8.

Attention to the word. This Scripture describes two types of wives. Which one are you? "An **excellent wife** is a *crown* of her husband, but **she who shames** him is as ***rottenness*** in his bones." Prov. 12:4. "He who gives **attention to the word** shall *find good*." Prov. 16:20.

Speak as a child. Have you matured? Or are you still a child who says things that hurt others? One of the biggest lies we learned as children was *Sticks and stones may break my bones, but words will never hurt me.* Many of us have never recovered from some of the words that were spoken to us as children. "When I was a child, I used to **speak as a child**, think as a child, reason as a child; when I became a man, I did away with *childish things*." 1Cor. 13:11.

Isn't it time for us to GROW UP? Stop saying things that hurt your husband, your children and your relationship with others!

Righteous lips. Who doesn't appreciate a kind word from someone? "**Righteous lips** are the *delight of kings,* and he who **speaks right** is *loved*." Prov. 16:13. "**Speaking** to one another in **psalms** and **hymns** and **spiritual songs**, singing and making melody with your heart to the Lord...." Eph. 5:19.

Abandon the quarrel. "The beginning of **strife** is like letting out water, so **abandon the quarrel** before it breaks out." Prov. 17:14. "A *fool's lips* bring **strife,** and his mouth calls for blows." Prov. 18:6. Again, **arguing** or **strife** is NOT GOOD for marriage (or any relationship) though others may tell you differently!

Constant friction. Is there constant friction in your home? "Deeds of the flesh are evident...**strife**, jealousy, **outbursts of anger**, **disputes, dissensions**, envying..." Gal. 5:19-21. "If any one advocates a different doctrine and **does not agree with sound words**, those of our *Lord Jesus Christ,* and with the **doctrine conforming to godliness**, he is conceited and understands nothing; but he has a morbid interest in controversial questions and **disputes** about words, out of which arise envy, **strife, abusive language**, evil suspicions, and **constant friction** between men of depraved mind and deprived of the truth...." 1Tim. 6:3-5.

AGREE QUICKLY! If you have problems with arguing, memorize these two verses. *These verses TOTALLY changed me!* "**Agree with thine adversary quickly**, while thou art in the way with him...." Matt. 5:25 KJV. "Keeping away from **strife** is an *honor* for a man, but any *fool* will **quarrel**." Prov. 20:3.

Two of you agree. You must try to find the area of *agreement* instead of the point of *disagreement* with EVERYTHING your husband says. If you can't find anything to agree about, KEEP

QUIET and smile! "Again I say to you, that if **two of you agree** on earth about anything that they may ask, it shall be done for them by My Father who is in heaven." Matt. 18:19.

Crushes the spirit. Proverbs also tells us that what we say can **crush** our husband's spirit! "A soothing tongue is a tree of life, but *perversion* (defined as "obstinacy") in it **crushes the spirit.**" Prov. 15:4.

Guard my mouth as with a muzzle. Here is a sobering thought: "Even before there is a word on my **tongue,** behold O Lord, *Thou dost know it all.*" Ps. 139:4. "I said, 'I will guard my ways, that I may *not sin* with my **tongue**; I will **guard my mouth as with a muzzle.**'" Ps. 39:1. Muzzle your tongue. Fasting is the ONLY way to be truly delivered from a big mouth! *Believe me, you're too weak to speak! It's what worked for me! Just do it – fast!*

Slander

Her husband safely trusts in her. Another area in which we must watch the way we speak, which can result in losing our husbands' trust, is in speaking about him to others. "The heart of her **husband safely trusts in her** and he will have no lack of gain" Prov. 31:7. We should *never* share our husbands' weaknesses or tell others something he told us in confidence. Remember that "A slanderer **separates intimate friends.**" Prov. 16:28. *So many women share with me (and with everyone else they know or meet) about their husband's sin of adultery, alcohol, drugs, or pornography. I REFUSE to listen and cut them right off.* Let me ask you, "How many people have *you* told?"

I will destroy! "Whoever secretly **slanders** his neighbor, him *I [God] will destroy.*" Ps. 101:5. So many women think that they are constantly battling the "enemy" when in fact it is God who is against them. If you have told others about your husband, you have slandered him. God promises that He will bring destruction in your life. You can rebuke the devil all you want, but Scripture is clear. You must repent and ask the Lord to remove this sin from your life and then make restitution by going back to everyone you have told. Confess your own sinfulness to them and then share all the good things your husband has done (and is doing) for you.

A slanderer reveals secrets. One of the most common snares that women fall into is gossiping over the telephone, under the guise of sharing "prayer concerns" or "prayer requests." Stop hanging around with women who gossip. Do as God commands: "...do NOT *associate* with a **gossip**." Prov. 20:19.

Slander be put away from you. Others may not realize that you're a gossip, but God knows your heart. Don't fool yourself; you don't need to get into details to share prayer concerns – you're a fool! "And he who spreads **slander** is a FOOL." Prov. 10:18. All of us must put sharing prayer requests, which is nothing more than slander, away from us. "Let all bitterness and wrath and anger and clamor and **slander be put away from you**, along with all malice." Eph. 4:31.

You may find as you get rid of this type of "sharing" that you have nothing to say to your friends. *It also resulted in my acquiring new friends!* If you resist the temptation to slide back into your old ways, God will be faithful to teach you to edify instead of shaming your husband. "An excellent wife is the crown of her husband, but she who **shames him** is as *rottenness to his bones*." Prov. 12:4. Let's instead begin "...speaking to one another in psalms, and hymns and spiritual songs, singing and making melody with your heart to the Lord." Eph. 5:19.

Sweetness of speech. If you have shamed your husband by what you have said to him or about him, or by your attitude, God is so faithful to offer the cure: "A **joyful heart** is good *medicine*, but a broken spirit dries up bones." Prov. 17:22. "**Pleasant words** are a *honeycomb, sweet to the soul* and *healing to the bones*." Prov. 16:24. "**Sweetness of speech** *increases persuasiveness*." Prov. 16:21.

God sees! Watching how much you say, winning your husband without a word and then getting out of your husband's way is what God's Word tells us to do. God is also adamant about the "attitude" behind our actions, since this shows our heart. "...for God *sees* not as man sees, for man looks at the outward appearance, but the LORD looks at the heart." 1Sam. 16:7. The attitude of a godly woman is one of respect for her husband, which stems from a pure heart.

Respectful

We are told that respect is something that we should *demand* from others. We are told that we should have respect for *ourselves*. To learn the true meaning of respect, let us look for a deeper understanding. Our husbands are to be won "by the behavior of their wives, as they observe [our] chaste and **respectful** behavior." 1Pet. 3:1. The word respect is defined in the dictionary as: "a special esteem or consideration in which one holds ***another*** person"! It is NOT what we demand for ourselves!

According to the thesaurus respect(ful) means having admiration, **considerate; to esteem, to honor, to reverence**, to admire, **to appreciate**, to notice, to prize, **to treasure**, to uphold, to value. Antonyms (the opposite) are **scorn, blame,** and **censure.** We will study the words in bold in more depth.

Consideration: thoughtfulness toward others. Hebrews tells us that we need to *encourage* our husbands and others. By our actions, we can stimulate them to love us and to also seek to do good. "And let us be **considerate** of how to *stimulate one another to love and good deeds*." Heb. 10:24. Therefore, when we are inconsiderate, we motivate our husbands or children to despise us and do wrong!

The deeds of the flesh. We use our husbands' sins to excuse our lack of respect for them. Here is a list of sins as stated in Galatians. As you read them, please take a moment to underline those sins that are usually committed by men, the ones that we in the church call *real* sin.

"Now the **deeds of the flesh** are evident, which are: immorality, impurity, sensuality, idolatry, sorcery, enmities (hostility), strife (contentions), jealousy, outbursts of anger, disputes, dissensions (differing opinion), factions (actions that cause friction), envying, drunkenness, carousing, and things like these, of which I forewarn you...that those who practice such things shall not inherit the kingdom of God." Gal. 5:19-21.

Now go back and circle the sins we tend to ignore in the church, those that are usually committed by women. To excuse your disrespect, based on your husband's sin(s), is obviously based on IGNORANCE or excusing your own sinfulness before a Holy God! We are clearly full of sin which God says is "evident"!

Looking to yourself. Many feel that it is their responsibility to punish or chastise others who sin, especially their own husbands. Scripture tells us differently and shows us the consequences of these prideful actions. Let us not forget the log in our own eye. Remember that all sins are the same to God.

Again, don't let Satan fool you into thinking that *your husband's* sin is worse than yours. "Brethren, even if a man is caught in *any trespass*, you who are spiritual, **restore** such a one *in a spirit of gentleness* (KJV **consideration**); each one **looking to yourself**, lest you too be tempted. Bear one another's burdens, and thus fulfill the law of Christ. For if anyone thinks he is something when he is nothing, he deceives himself." Gal. 6:1-3.

Esteem: high regard *for others*. Many Christian psychologists have taken God's command "to esteem others better than ourselves" and twisted it to teach us to build up ourselves, rather than others. Read this entire passage to allow the truth to set you free from esteem and pride, which is destroying you and your marriage:

"Let **nothing** be done through strife or vain glory; but in lowliness of mind let each **esteem** OTHERS *better than* **themselves**. Do not look out for your own interests, but for the interests of others. Have the attitude in yourselves which was also in Christ Jesus, who, although He existed in the form of God, did not regard equality with God a thing to be grasped, but emptied Himself, taking the form of a bond-servant, and being made in the likeness of men." Phil 2:3-7.

Appreciate those who have charge over you. Your husband has charge over you. Did you make his job easier or harder? "We request of you, brethren, that you **appreciate** those who diligently labor among you and have charge over you...and that you **esteem** them very highly in love because of their work. Live in peace with one another." 1Thes. 5:13.

Honor: regard highly. We are to regard our husbands as worthy of honor, honor we should *already* be showing them. "Let all who are under the yoke as slaves regard their own masters as worthy of all **honor** so that the name of God and our doctrine may not be spoken against." 1Tim 6:1.

God may not be dishonored. Remember that by showing honor to your husband, whether or not his actions warrant or deserve honor, you bring glory to God! Not only when your husband is around, but at all times in your speaking of him and in your thoughts of him. The consequence of not showing this type of respect is dishonor to God and His Word. We say we are Christians but our "deeds deny" it! (Titus 1:16) "...to be...kind, being subject to their own husbands, that the word of **God may not be dishonored.**" Titus 2:5. And "Wives be subject to your own husbands, **as to the Lord.**" Eph. 5:22.

In toil. "Then to Adam He said, 'Because you have listened to the voice of your wife, and have eaten from the tree about which I commanded you, saying, "You shall not eat from it"; Cursed is the ground because of you; **In toil** you shall eat of it all the days of your life.'" Gen. 3:17. After the fall of man, the man and the woman were each given a punishment; the woman would have pain in childbirth and the man would have to toil on the ground or work. So why is the man's punishment now shared by both the man and the woman? Why did we buy into this lie? Pride.

A woman full of pride doesn't want to be told what to do or how she should spend money. If she makes her own money then she can make her own decisions about how her money is to be spent! We can easily slip out from under our husbands' authority and ultimately their protection as well.

In addition, when wives have a different career than that of the home and children, it divides the couple's interests and makes us independent of each other. God warns us when He says that a house that is divided will not stand! Has your job or career destroyed your marriage? (See "The Ways of Her Household" in *A Wise Woman Builds Her House: By a FOOL Who Tore Hers Down with Her Own Hands*.)

Grant her honor. All women long to have our husbands treat us as in the following verse: "You husbands likewise, live with your wives in an understanding way, as with a weaker vessel, since she is a woman; and **grant her honor** as a fellow heir of the grace of life, so that your prayers may not be hindered." 1Pet. 3:7. By striving to be quiet and gentle, and to honor our husbands, especially when they may be living dishonorably, in a chaste and respectful manner, we can receive the blessing of having our husbands honor us by choosing to return home!

Here are some Scriptural guidelines on how to receive the honor:

By being gracious. "A *gracious woman* receives **honor**." Prov. 11:16. Respond graciously to WHATEVER is said to you ALWAYS with all people! Never press or overreact! Remember, you are a child of the King – act like royalty! Those in royalty never show ill emotions or fly off in a rage. Think of Princess Di who was experiencing all kinds of horrible marital pain, yet you never saw her pitch a fit or make a scene.

By having humility. "And before **honor** comes humility." Prov. 15:33.

By being humble. "But humility goes before **honor**." Prov. 18:12.

Reverence: a feeling of *great* **respect**, love, awe, and esteem; to fear. Many women do not respect or show reverence to their husbands.

How can we as Christian women ignore the Scriptures? "And let the wife see to it that she **respect** her husband." In the King James Version it says, "And the wife see that she **reverence** her husband." Eph. 5:33.

Appreciate: to give favorable recognition; to cherish, enjoy, value, understand; to treasure (especially in the marriage vow), to take loving care of, to keep alive (in emotion). We spoke about doing things from the heart. If your husband is not one of your treasures, your heart is not with him. "For where your **treasure** is there will be your *heart* also." Matt. 6:21.

Sometimes when we lose something or temporarily misplace it, we then realize how important it is to us. Did it take losing your husband for you to realize what you had? *I know it did with me!*

How can you help heal your husband spiritually and emotionally? Speak sweetly and gently to your husband whenever the Lord gives you an opportunity to speak to him. "A **soothing tongue** is a tree of life, but perversion in it crushes the spirit." Prov. 15:4.

This blessing can be yours. "All the days of the afflicted are bad, but a **cheerful heart** has a *continual feast*." Prov. 15:15. If your heart is cheerful, you will draw your husband back home, since he left to find happiness. When he leaves where he is now, will he find joy back in his own home with you and your children?

Here is a caution. Watch what you say about your husband. **Shame** is an emotional cancer. "An excellent wife is a crown to her husband, but she who **shames** him is as *rottenness in his bones*." Prov. 12:4. Rottenness is defined as decay by caries; decay as by *worm eating*. "In the end she (the harlot) is *bitter* as **wormwood**, sharp as a two-edged sword." Prov. 5:4.

A good word. NEVER talk to your husband about your troubles, fears or anxiety over his sins (adultery, abuse, alcohol or drugs), about your finances or about the impending divorce, since "**Anxiety in the heart** of a man weighs it down, but a *good word* makes it glad." Prov. 12:25. Whenever your husband happens to speak to you, he MUST leave feeling uplifted, not confronted or downtrodden.

Brings healing. Your tongue can have two opposing effects; which will you choose? "There is one who speaks rashly like the thrusts of a sword, but the *tongue of the wise* **brings healing**." Prov. 12:18.

A joyful heart. Have a joyful or a merry heart. "A **joyful heart** is *good medicine,* but a *broken spirit* dries up the bones." Prov. 17:22.

Cheerful face. Let your face show the joy that is in your heart. "A **joyful heart** makes a **cheerful face**, but when the heart is sad, the *spirit is broken.*" Prov. 15:13. Joyful is from the NAS; merry is from the KJV. Let's learn more about being joyful and merry. Merry: glad, **joyful, rejoicing.** Joyful: (to be) a good woman, pleasant, precious, sweet, **grateful, agreeable.**

Rejoice ALWAYS. In our circumstances it seems impossible to be happy. How can we possibly be merry or joyful? "**Rejoice** *in the Lord* **always**, again I say **rejoice.**" Phil 4:4. And when are we to rejoice? "**Rejoice** ALWAYS." 1Thes. 5:16. It's in Him that we rejoice. This is the MOST powerful weapon of our spiritual warfare – PRAISING the Lord when adversity comes against us!!

Are you able to do anything without murmuring and complaining? Do you complain, whine or murmur continually about your situation to others or your husband? If you do, you are not grateful! "Do **ALL** *things* without **murmuring and complaining.**" Phil. 2:14.

Have you learned the secret? We may think that in our circumstances we have reason to whine. Instead, we must learn to be content. "...for I have *learned* to be **content** in **whatever circumstances** I am. I know how to get along with humble means...and in any and **every circumstance** I have **learned the secret** of being filled and going hungry, both of having abundance and suffering need." Phil. 4:11-12.

Antonyms of Respect Are
Scorn, Blame and/or Censure

Did you scorn your husband? Did you blame him for past failures? Did you censure where he went or what he said? Now is the time to RENEW your mind. Read and reread this chapter until you've worn out the pages and have broken the binding. Make 3x5 cards for every Scripture verse that brought conviction in your spirit. Keep them with you in your purse and read them throughout the day. "Be diligent to present yourself approved to God as a workman who does not need to be ashamed, handling accurately the word of truth." 2Tim. 2:15.

In conclusion. Let us all first strive to appear wise by keeping silent. Next let us make sure that when we do open our mouths it is with wisdom, kindness, respect and edification. Let our words be sweet and gentle. Let us be a "crown" to our husbands in the way we handle this adversity in our lives, which will be "precious" in the sight of God!

Personal commitment: to open my mouth with wisdom and kindness. "Based on what I have learned from God's Word, I commit to remain quiet, wait before I answer and be sweet in my every word. I also commit to demonstrate a respectful attitude toward my husband because of the example it sets for others and the honor it gives to God and His Word."

Date: _____ Signed:_____

Chapter

8

Won Without a Word

*"In the same way (as Jesus) you wives
be submissive to your own husbands,
so that if any of them are
disobedient to the word,
they may be won without a word..."*
1 Peter 3:1

In this chapter, we will learn from God's Word that since our husbands are over us, our words are not only useless, but may be dangerous. Many of us are now reaping "bad fruits" of unknowingly trying to persuade or warn our husbands instead of taking our concerns to God. We will learn that everything that you'd like to say to your husband, you must first talk to God about.

When our husbands are doing something against God's Word, we are told in Scripture to win our husbands "without a word," with a respectful attitude toward them and their God-given authority over us.

Won Without a Word

When I am concerned about something, should I discuss it with my husband? No.

Ask God to speak to your husband. We must not discuss our fears or concerns or even our desires with our husbands. Instead, we must first go to the top; we must go to Our Heavenly Father and appeal to Him. Ask God to have the Lord speak to your husband (since the Lord is directly over ALL men) about what is on your heart.

This is the proper order of authority: "But I want you to understand that Christ is the head of **every** man, and the man is the head of woman, and God is the head of Christ." 1Cor. 11:3. Instead of seeking your husband's help or guidance, you must seek the face of God. Then search the Scriptures for one of God's principles concerning the dilemma you face. This will confirm what the Lord has spoken to you in your heart. Mark that verse and then hold onto it, KNOWING that the Lord is in control.

Get out of His Way!

Get out of his way. "How blessed is the man who does not walk in the counsel of the wicked, **nor stand in the way of sinners**...But his delight is in the law of the Lord, And in His law he meditates day and night." Psalm 1:1 NIV. Get out of your husband's way; you are not his authority! The second line tells us what we are **to do**; meditate on His Word and leave your husband to God. God must be the One to change your husband; your husband can't even change himself.

Stand in the way. "How blessed is the man who does not walk in the counsel of the wicked, nor **stand in the WAY** of sinners, nor sit in the seat of scoffers!" Ps. 1:1. When dealing with a husband who is "disobedient to the word" there must be stages of "letting go" **without a word**. A woman whose husband is in the home, but is not coming home on time or at all, must "let go" of trying to police him through curfews, "20 questions" or the "silent treatment."

If a wife finds out that her husband is involved with another woman, she must "let go" by not following him or confronting him and use this time as a "wake-up call" or she will push him into leaving or divorcing her. If at this stage he leaves, and she continues to stand in his way rather than "letting go," he will most likely push the divorce through, hoping that this will stop his wife's pursuits. However, if she still pursues, then you will see the man marry the other woman. (For more information we have two excellent Q & A videos "Alluring and Unconditional Love" and "Contentment to Unleash a Miracle.")

If she still holds on, rather than "letting go," then you will most likely see her former husband in a VERY strong second marriage. I have personally known women whose husbands had remarried, yet who were still signing their husband's name to Christmas cards and thank you notes! In addition, with this distorted view of their situation, they have no qualms about continuing to be sexually intimate. Rarely do you see a divorce occur when a husband is convinced that he can basically have two wives.

Very often a wife who won't let go will see her former husband and his new wife resort to having a child of their own, hoping this will discourage the ex-wife and make her let go. Some women write to me in a rage and anger against God because He did not close the OW's womb. Yet they neglect to acknowledge that they failed to follow the Biblical principles of letting go and obtaining a gentle and quiet spirit. Occasionally, when a husband does divorce the OW or second wife, he doesn't go back to his first wife, but instead searches for someone new to make him happy! (For encouragement, please read the testimony at the end of Chapter 12 "Asking God" about a woman who humbly let her husband go, did NOT get angry at God, and found herself with a restored marriage after her husband remarried!)

Get off his back and pray! You can help to heal your home by your prayers. "Therefore, confess your sins to one another, and **pray** for one another, so that you may be healed. The effective **prayer** of a righteous man can accomplish much." Jas. 5:16. If you do speak, then it is VERY important that you choose your words carefully!

Turn, THROUGH PRAYER ALONE, your husband's direction to God. You must understand also that you are not responsible for what your husband does; he is accountable to God for his actions. "But each one is **tempted** when he is carried away and enticed by his *own lust*." Jas. 1:14. Close your mouth; then get out of your husband's way.

Wives love to treat their husbands as if they were one of their children. This type of mothering attitude will drive off *any* man and drain the manliness out of him. Then when a woman comes along who looks to him as the man, he leaves his wife for the other woman.

Have the proper attitude. "Let every person be in subjection to the governing authorities. For **there is no authority except from God**, and those which exist are established by God. Therefore he who resists authority has opposed the ordinance of God; and they who have opposed will receive condemnation upon themselves." Rom. 13:1.

Your husband is your God-ordained authority. Your rebellion to his authority has allowed your present situation. Obey and submit NOW and watch God turn your husband's heart back home as you honor God's Word.

Overcome all evil with good. Your reaction to the evil *when* it occurs tells God, others who are watching and your husband what is REALLY in your heart. "Do not be *overcome with evil* but **overcome evil with good**." Rom. 12:21. It **will** occur but you can be prepared, "...knowing that the **testing of your faith** produces *endurance*." Jas. 1:3.

Take this opportunity to speak a blessing of kindness to your husband: "...not returning evil for evil, or insult for insult, but *giving a blessing instead*; for you were called for the very purpose that you might inherit a blessing." 1Pet. 3:9. If you agree with the insult or hurtful statement and then return a kind statement or blessing, this will turn your situation around in an INSTANT!

However, most women spend their energy defending themselves or discussing the issue. As they attempt to get their spouse to take *his* responsibility for what happened, they fail to see their situation improve. "HE WAS LED AS A SHEEP TO SLAUGHTER; AND AS A LAMB BEFORE ITS SHEARER IS SILENT, SO HE DOES NOT OPEN HIS MOUTH." Acts 8:32.

These are the women who e-mail me wanting to know what is stopping their restoration. But when I hear their derogatory and condescending attitude, I know why! Can you humbly accept what I am saying? If you can't, do you wonder why your husband has chosen to leave you? "The wise woman builds her house, But the foolish tears it down with her own hands." Prov. 14:1.

(For encouragement, please read the testimony at the end of Chapter 12, "Asking God" about a woman who humbly let her husband go, did NOT get angry at God, and found herself with a restored marriage after her husband remarried!)

Concentrate on loving the unlovable! When you love and respect your husband, even when he is unlovable, unkind and in sin, you are showing him unconditional love. "For if you love those who love you, what reward have you? Do not even the tax-gatherers do the same?" Matt. 5:46. Give God your hurts. He will help you love your husband if you just *ask* Him.

The ministry of reconciliation. As children of God we are to be ambassadors of God's love and that will draw others to the Lord. "Therefore we are **ambassadors FOR Christ**...(Christ) gave us the **ministry of reconciliation**...*not counting their trespasses against them*, and he has committed the word of reconciliation." 2Cor. 5:18-20.

Have you been counting? Do you rehearse your husband's sins and shortcomings in your mind as you reveal his trespasses to others? Remember, God's mercies are new every morning – are yours?

Our first mission field. Your attitude may be, "Why should I minister to my husband the sinner?" Because the Lord gives us *our* husbands and our children as our first "mission field" before we can truly be effective with others.

We, of course, want to rush ahead of God before we are really ready and minister to those in the church, in the neighborhood and at work – while we neglect our ministry **at home**! If you haven't won your husband or children to the Lord, how can you win the lost?

So many women act like victims having to live with an unbeliever. Yet, they are the very ones keeping their husbands or children from the Lord. A Pharisee who attends services and then acts arrogant and spiritual keeps the lost from wanting a relationship with the Lord! Is this you?

God wants us to learn contentment BEFORE He'll change our husbands. If you are still whining and bemoaning your situation, then be prepared to stay in it! We can see in Paul's life: "Not that I speak from want; for I have **learned to be content** in whatever circumstances I am. I know how to get along with humble means, and I also know how to live in prosperity; in any and every circumstance I have **learned the secret** of being filled and going hungry, both of having abundance and suffering need."

Paul goes on to say (the verse you hear so often), "I can do all things through Him who strengthens me." Phil. 4:11-13. You will stay in difficulty until you have LEARNED contentment in it – period!

Uniquely Created

Created for the man. Women, it is important that we seek the wisdom, knowledge and understanding from God's Word to fully appreciate how we were created and why we were created. 1Cor. 11:8-9 says, "For man does not originate from woman, but woman from man; for indeed man was not created for the woman's sake, but **woman for the man's sake.**" Gen. 2:20.

As we begin to move into God's perfect plan for our lives, we then can live the abundant life God promises in His Word. Our lives will reflect God's Word, rather than denying it. And most importantly, others will be drawn to Christ through the testimony of our lives.

Helper suitable for him. "And the man gave names to all the cattle, and to the birds of the sky, and to every beast of the field, but for Adam there was not found a **helper suitable for him**." These statements really get under the skin of the feminists. Does it get under yours too?

Woman independent of man. "However, in the Lord, neither is **woman independent of man**, nor is man independent of woman. For as the woman originates from the man, so also the man has his birth through the woman; and all things originate from God." 1Cor. 11:11-12.

God created men and women with different needs. The voids in our lives and in our husbands lives create a type of working gear (or puzzle pieces if you will). As we fill our voids ourselves or apart from our husbands, the gear slips. The more we fill our needs or the more our husbands fill their needs independently from the marriage, our relationship slips until there is nothing left to hang on to.

Feminists have pushed the majority of us to fulfill our own needs and let our husbands fend for themselves. We have believed the lie that it is not good to be dependent on each other. The coined phrase "codependent" encourages many to pull away instead of cherishing being one flesh. God created a void in each of us that only our spouse can (or should) fill. If being codependent is wrong, then how do excuse this verse? "However, in the Lord, *neither* is **woman independent of man**, *nor* is **man independent of woman**. For as the woman originates from the man, so also the man has his birth through the woman; and all things originate from God." 1Cor. 11:11-12.

As Christians, we must renew our mind to line up with God's Word. God's Word is truth! "And do not be conformed to this world, but be transformed by the renewing of your mind, that you may prove what the will of God is, that which is good and acceptable and perfect." Rom. 12:2. Living the truth certainly will not be easy and it will almost seem crazy at first to those who observe the change in you. But through obedience to His Word, we will soon understand and reap the rewards of our obedience. We as Christians obey and believe, even when we don't see the change or understand the command. This is the faith we profess as believers.

We have all experienced how the world's way has worn us out because we have tried to do something we weren't created to do and act in a way we were NOT designed to act. So let's look first at how and why we were created in the beginning.

Many of us want to be such good helpers that we do everything for our husbands and actually rob him of blessings or rip the manliness out of him. We do, do, do. We make the decisions, do everything around the house and in the yard and help provide part of the income. We then are surprised that with all his free time, he finds himself another woman who appears to need and really want him.

Begin to look at the roles God created as special and unique. Ask the Lord for guidance and discernment in each task you are presently undertaking. If you have taken something your husband should be doing, pray that the Lord will change it. Many times it is some mini catastrophe that your husband must rescue you from that will bring about the change. But don't you cause a crisis on purpose: wait for the Lord; stop manipulating!

It doesn't matter if your husband is not in the home either. Hundreds of women have sought the Lord in this area to find their husbands taking over the finances, car maintenance or replacement, the yard, home repairs, etc. NEVER underestimate God!!

Personal commitment: to pray to our Father rather than to quickly speak to our husbands. "Based on what I have learned from God's Word, I commit to allowing God to move my husband through His Holy Spirit. I will instead 'bathe all my desires and concerns in prayer' by seeking His face. I acknowledge that the only way to win my husband to righteousness, especially in my present circumstances, is 'without a word,' and with my respectful and humble spirit."

Date: _____ Signed:_____

Chapter

9

A Gentle and Quiet Spirit

*"But let it be the
hidden person of the heart,
with the imperishable quality of a
gentle and quiet spirit,
which is precious in the sight of God."*
1 Peter 3:4

Boisterous women are common today. Boisterous is defined as "offensively loud and insistent." It is not only accepted but encouraged through our media.

Sadly, this behavior has also permeated the church and Christians today. Is it any wonder that the divorce rate is now higher in the church than the national average?

A woman with a "gentle and quiet spirit" is called a doormat. She is told that her husband won't respect her if she doesn't stand up for herself.

Husbands even tell their own wives to fight back or defend themselves, and at the same time they follow through with the divorce and stay with the other woman. God said that a gentle and quiet spirit is precious to Him, and therefore is the only way toward healing and restoration.

However, when a husband strays from the truth and falls into sin, you hear Christians, even pastors, advise the wife to use "tough love" even though it is unbiblical and destroys marriages. In addition, it results in a "hardened heart" which inevitably results in a wife who is unwilling or unable to forgive her husband. Only a heart of flesh, a tender heart, is able to truly forgive.

In this chapter we will seek the truth regarding tough love and the healing that comes through forgiveness.

Tough Love?

Love is patient. God gives us a description of love. See if you can find the word "tough" or any word even remotely similar. "**Love is patient,** love is kind, and is not jealous; love does not brag and is not arrogant, does not act unbecomingly; it does not seek its own, is **not provoked, does not take into account a wrong suffered,** does not rejoice in unrighteousness, but rejoices with the truth; bears all things, believes all things, hopes all things, endures all things. Love never fails...." 1Cor. 13:4-8.

This verse proves that there is no place for "tough love" in a marriage, on either side. The love that Jesus lived and calls us to is "tough" to live, but never "tough" in response to another whom we love.

This I command you. Another very popular statement in the church today is "Love is a choice." Read with me the following verse to see if God says we can "choose" to love. Or does God **command** that we do so, as followers of Christ? "This I **command** you, that you **love one another.**" John 15:17. We do have a choice: to obey His **command** or not. This is not exactly what Christian psychologists are telling us, is it?

Love your enemies. Our friends encourage us to "protect ourselves" or to "not love those who are difficult to love." Are we to love them or not? "But I say to you who hear, **love your enemies,** do good to those who hate you, bless those who curse you, pray for those who mistreat you." Luke 6:27-28.

In this passage God is even clearer. He even admonishes those who only love the lovable: "But I say to you, **love your enemies,** and pray for those who persecute you...for **if you love those who love you,** what reward have you? Do not even the tax-gatherers do the same?" Matt. 5:44-46.

Leave room for the wrath of God. In the book that talks to us about being "tough" with our spouse, we are told to confront, to cause a crisis. In other words, we are to take matters into our own hands. What does God instruct us to do? "...rejoicing in hope, persevering in tribulation, devoted to prayer...Bless those who persecute you; bless and curse not...Never pay back evil for evil to anyone. Respect what is right in the sight of all men. If possible, so far as it depends on you, be at peace with all men. Never take your own revenge, beloved, but **leave room for the wrath of God**, for it is written, 'VENGEANCE IS MINE, I WILL REPAY,' says the Lord." Rom. 12:12,14,17-19.

He uttered no threats. You may ask yourself "Why do I have to endure such suffering, and not even have the satisfaction of vengeance?" Read God's explanation for your suffering.

"For you have been called for this purpose, since Christ also suffered for you, leaving you an example for you to follow in His steps...and while being reviled, **He did not revile in return**; while suffering, **He uttered no threats**, but kept entrusting Himself to Him (God) who judges righteously." 1Pet. 2:21-23.

Overcome evil with good. "But if your enemy is hungry, feed him, and if he is thirsty, give him a drink, for in so doing you will heap burning coals upon his head; Do not be overcome by evil, but **overcome evil with good**." Rom. 12:20-21.

Blessed are the meek. If you don't take matters into your own hands and take a "tough" stand, others (even Christians), will tell you that you are a doormat. However, let me remind you who Jesus said are "blessed": "**Blessed are the meek**, for they shall inherit the earth." Matt. 5:5. Jesus chose to lay down His life and allowed His enemies to seize Him. Are we to follow in His steps or not?

The righteousness of God. People may even remind you about when Jesus turned over the tables in the Temple. They will use this example to tell you that you have the "right" to be angry with others. God says He is a jealous God. Can we then also be jealous? "But let everyone be quick to hear, slow to speak, and slow to anger; for **the anger of man does NOT achieve the righteousness of God**." Jas. 1:19-20.

That you may not do the things that you please. When we have an impulse to do or say something to another that is anything but meek, then we are walking in the flesh and not in the Spirit. "But I say, walk in the Spirit, and you will not carry out the desire of the flesh.

"For the flesh sets its desire against the Spirit, and the Spirit against the flesh; for these are in opposition to one another, so **that you may not do the things that you please**. But the fruit of the Spirit is love, joy, peace, patience, kindness, goodness, faithfulness, gentleness, self-control." Gal. 5:16,17, 22-23. "And just as you want people to treat you, **treat them in the same way.**" Luke 6:31.

The kindness of God. It is deception to think that confronting and being unkind and firm will turn the other person around. If that worked, why would God use kindness to draw us to repentance? Sinners do not go forward to accept the Lord because they think that they are going to be criticized or chastised, do they? "Or do you think lightly of the riches of His kindness and forbearance and patience, not knowing that **the kindness of God** leads you to repentance?" Rom. 2:4.

No one will see the Lord. Another extremely important reason for your gentle and quiet spirit in dealing with your husband (or others) is that we are to let others see Christ in us. "Pursue peace with all men, and the sanctification without which **no one will see the Lord.**" Heb. 12:14.

Don't think that you can act kindly with your husband, but act horribly with your children, parents or coworkers. God is watching and He is the one who will turn your husband's heart. Nothing is hidden from Him. Let us not forget that He is looking at our hearts; therefore, even if you try to control your anger, He is looking deeper! You must "die to self."

The ministry of reconciliation. We are to be ambassadors for Christ in reconciliation. "Now all these things are from God, who reconciled us to Himself through Christ, and gave us **the ministry of reconciliation**, namely, that God was in Christ reconciling the world to Himself, not counting their trespasses against them, and He has committed to us the word of reconciliation.

"Therefore, we are **ambassadors** for Christ, as though God were entreating through us; we **beg you** on behalf of Christ, be reconciled to God." 2Cor. 5:18-20.

Lest you too be tempted. The following Scripture is a warning to us when we are not gentle to others when they have sinned against us. "Brethren, even if a man is caught in any trespass, you who are spiritual, restore such a one in a spirit of gentleness; each one looking to yourself, **lest you too be tempted**. Bear one another's burdens, and thus fulfill the law of Christ." Gal. 6:1-2.

Lest the Lord see it and be displeased. Many women have been so happy to see their husbands "get what they deserve" when God punishes them with financial difficulties or other trials. Then they see their husbands' situation turn around for the better. Why does this happen? "Do not rejoice when your enemy falls, and do not let your heart be glad when he stumbles; lest the **Lord see it and be displeased**, and He turn away His anger from him." Prov. 24:17.

Doers of the Word. It's important that we learn the truth and agree with what we see in Scripture, but we must not stop there. "But prove yourselves **doers of the word**, and not merely hearers who delude themselves...not having become a forgetful hearer but an effectual doer, this man shall be blessed in what he does." Jas. 1:22, 25. "Therefore, to him who **knows the right thing to do**, and does not do it, to him it is sin." Jas. 4:17.

The error of unprincipled men. God has warned us that we should not listen to or follow men who tell us something contrary to Scripture. "Be diligent to be found by Him in peace, spotless and blameless, and regard the patience of our Lord to be salvation; just as also our beloved brother Paul, according to the wisdom given him...in which are some things hard to understand, which the untaught and unstable distort, as they do also the rest of Scripture, to their own destruction. You therefore, beloved, knowing this beforehand, be on your guard lest, being **carried away by the error of unprincipled men,** you fall from your own steadfastness, but grow in the grace and knowledge of our Lord Jesus Christ...." 2Pet. 3:14-18.

Tough love is wrong and totally contradicts the teachings and example of Jesus. Let us instead **learn** from Him who describes Himself as "gentle and humble in heart." "Take My yoke upon you, and learn from Me, for I am gentle and humble in heart; and you shall find rest for your souls. For My yoke is easy, and My load is light." Matt. 11:29.

Forgiveness

Only a woman with a heart that is gentle and quiet can forgive her husband. However, many women have been deceived and do not forgive their husbands because they don't fully understand the grave consequences of their lack of forgiveness. Let's search the Scriptures to see what God says about forgiving others. Here are some questions we should ask:

Q. Why should I forgive my husband or the others involved?

Christ also has forgiven you. We forgive because God forgave us. "And be kind to one another, tender-hearted, forgiving each other, just as God in **Christ also has forgiven you**." Eph. 4:32.

The precious blood of the covenant. Jesus shed His blood for the forgiveness of sins – even your husband's sin! "All things are cleansed with blood, and without the shedding of blood there is no forgiveness." Heb. 9:22 "For this is my blood of the covenant, which is poured out for many **for forgiveness of sins**." Matt. 26:28.

Reaffirm your love for him. To relieve the offender's sorrow. "...You should rather forgive and **comfort him**, lest somehow such a one be overwhelmed by excessive sorrow. Wherefore I *urge you* to **reaffirm your love for him**." 2Cor. 2:7-8.

Let no advantage be taken of us by Satan. Satan can use a lack of forgiveness against you to take the advantage. "For if indeed what I have forgiven...I did it for your sakes in the presence of Christ, in order that **no advantage be taken of us by Satan**; for we are not ignorant of his schemes." 2Cor. 2:10-11.

Our Father will not forgive *YOUR* transgressions. God said that He won't forgive us if we don't forgive others. "For if you forgive men for their transgressions, your heavenly Father will also forgive you, but if you do not forgive men, then **your Father will not forgive *your* transgressions**." Matt. 6:14-15. "So shall My heavenly Father also do to you, if each of you do not forgive his brother *from your heart*." Matt. 18:35.

Q. But shouldn't the offender be sorry if I'm to forgive?

Father, forgive them. Those who crucified Jesus never asked forgiveness; nor were they sorry for what they were doing or what they had done. If we are Christians, we are followers of Christ; therefore we are to follow His example. "**Father, forgive them, for they know not what they are doing.**" Luke 23:34.

When Stephen was being stoned he cried out just before he died, "**Lord, do not hold this sin against them!**" Acts 7:60. Could *you* do any less?!

Q. But how often does God expect me to forgive?

Seventy times seven. Many women exclaim, "But *my* husband has done this to me before, throughout our entire marriage!" When Peter asked how often he was to forgive, Jesus said to him, "I do not say to you, up to seven times, but up to **seventy times seven**." Matt. 18:22. That's 490 times for the same offense!

Remember no more. Does forgiveness really mean that I forget that sin, even in an argument, even in divorce? "For I will forgive their iniquity, and their sin I will **remember no more**." Jer. 31:34. "As far as the east is from the west, so far has He removed our transgressions from us." Ps. 103:12. "Not returning evil for evil, or insult for insult, but giving a blessing instead; for you were called for the very purpose that you might inherit a blessing." 1Pet. 3:9.

Be prepared; Satan will try to bring up old transgressions in your mind even after you have forgiven. When he does you must forgive again. Many women whose husbands have been unfaithful to them, even after their husbands have returned home have experienced "flashbacks," almost like "spiritual" war trauma. They say they must continually, sometimes daily, forgive.

Q. How can I possibly forgive as God has asked me to do in His Word?

God alone. Only God can help you to do it. You must *humble* yourself and ask Him to give you the grace. "*Who can forgive sins but **God alone**?*" Mark 2:7.

Ask. "...You do not have because you do not ask." James 4:2. Ask God to forgive your husband through you as you yield to Him. (For more help on how you can really forgive your husband, get our testimony tape to hear how God did it for me!)

God gives grace to the humble. How do I get the grace I need? "God is opposed to the proud but **gives grace to the humble**. Humble yourselves therefore under the mighty hand of God that He may exalt you at the proper time." 1Pet. 5:5-6.

Humbled their heart. How can I gain humility? "Because they had rebelled against the words of God and spurned the counsel of the Most High. Therefore He **humbled their heart** *with labor*; they stumbled and there was none to help.

"Then they cried out to the Lord in their trouble; He saved them out of their distresses." Ps. 107:11-13. "I **humbled my soul** *with fasting*; and my *prayer* kept returning to my bosom." Ps. 35:13. Sometimes it could be through illness that He quiets and humbles you. Don't fight it – it's God working.

First be reconciled to your brother. When do I need to forgive those who have hurt me? Shouldn't I feel convicted of it first? "If therefore you are presenting your offering at the altar, and there remember that your brother has something against you, leave your offering there before the altar, and go your way; **first be reconciled to your brother**, and then come and present your offering." Matt. 5:23-24. If you have not forgiven another, especially your husband, you need to ask forgiveness.

Bitterness. Not forgiving someone causes bitterness. The definition of bitterness is "poison!" "Let all **bitterness** and wrath and anger...be put away from you." Eph 4:31. Not forgiving another is eating at you, not the other person! "The heart knows its own bitterness." Prov. 14:10. "For He knows the secrets of the heart." Ps. 44:21.

A brother offended. Be sure that you follow Scriptural guidelines. I have heard many who have said that things were actually worse when they did ask forgiveness or that it did no good. I can speak from experience. At times, when I have asked for another's forgiveness, I have stated it the wrong way and further offended the other person. "**A brother offended** is harder to be won than a strong city." Prov. 18:19.

Men pleasers. Be mindful that you may fool your husband but God knows your motives and your heart. "...but the Lord looks at the heart." 1Sam. 16:7. "...In the sincerity of your heart, as to Christ; not by way of eyeservice, as **men pleasers**, but as slaves of Christ, doing the will of God from the heart." Eph 6:5-6.

Every idle word. Prepare *every word you say*! Every word you say must be carefully chosen. "A fool does not delight in understanding, but only in revealing his own mind." Prov. 18:2. "**Every idle word** that men shall speak they *shall give an account* thereof in the day of judgment." Matt. 12:36.

Try writing down what you are going to say. Then read out loud what you wrote, putting yourself in the other person's shoes and hearing it from his point of view. Did it sound accusing? Ask God to put the right words in your mouth and speak through you.

Many words. "When there are **many words**, transgression is unavoidable." Prov. 10:19. Only say what *you* did; don't set the stage with something like, *When you did this, and such and such, well then I....*

He uttered no threats. If the other person starts to lash out at you, do not open your mouth except to agree. "And while being reviled, He did not revile in return; while suffering **He uttered no threats**...." 1Pet. 2:23.

Every idle word. The Prodigal Son prepared his words after his decision to return home: "I will get up and go to my father, and will say to him, '**Father I have sinned** against heaven, and in your sight; I am no longer worthy to be called your son; make me as one of your hired men.' " Luke 15:18-19.

Make sure your words are sweet and kind EVERY TIME you have an opportunity to see your husband! Remember, "Sweetness of speech adds persuasiveness." Prov. 16:21. And, "Pleasant words are a honeycomb, **sweet to the soul** and **healing** to the bones." Prov. 16:24.

Q. How can I be sure I have truly forgiven?

You will know and have the confidence that you have truly forgiven when your sin and weaknesses loom before your eyes so large that you are unable to see your husband's sins and weaknesses. You will be blind to his past, present and future failings.

When women write or talk about ANYTHING that their husband is doing wrong, then I know that they are far from restoration. So many who have been seeking restoration see no progress because they have failed to take the full responsibility for the sins committed in the marriage that caused the separation, divorce or adultery.

They, in error, want to "share" their part in it, which is to their own destruction. Jesus took the full and complete responsibility and bore ALL of our sins. We, too, must take all and bear all. Then, as believers, we can seek the Lord and lay the sins of the marriage at the foot of the cross, knowing the debt has been paid.

Personal commitment: to desire and strive to be gentle and quiet. "Based on what I have learned in Scripture, I commit to do everything I have learned by being quick to hear and slow to speak; to forgive those who have offended me and to do what I can to reconcile with those I have offended."

Date: _____ Signed:_____

10

He Turns the Heart

*"The king's heart is like channels of water
in the hand of the Lord;
He turns it wherever He wishes."
Proverbs 21:1*

Has everyone told you that your husband has his own will; therefore, he may "choose" not to return to you?

When trying to restore your marriage you will be bombarded, as other women have, by the onslaught of those who will tell you that it is your husband's choice and his "free will" to choose to leave you or to be with another woman. I faced the exact same response, especially from pastors. But, praise the Lord, He showed me the truth!!!

The key is not your husband's will, but **God's** will! And when seeking God's will He showed me that it was His will to turn my husband's heart back to me, his wife, because it is what He joined together. Glory to God!!!

Let me show you what He showed me:

It's NOT Man's Will but God's Will!!

"He does **His** *will*...." Dan. 4:31

"He bestows it on whomever **He** wishes...." Dan. 4:25

"**God** is able to deliver...." Dan 3:17

Consider Nebuchadnezzar. After his pride caused him to crawl like an animal, he said of God, "He does according to His will in the host of heaven and among the inhabitants of earth; And no one can ward off His hand or say to Him, 'What hast Thou done?' " Dan. 4:35. Is this not the same God who still does according to His will? Is your husband greater than King Nebuchadnezzar?

Consider also Jonah. Jonah was unwilling to do what God wanted him to do, but God *made* him willing. "And the Lord appointed a great fish to swallow Jonah, and Jonah was in the stomach of the fish three days and three nights." Jonah 1:17. God is MORE THAN ABLE to make your husband willing!!

Lastly, consider Paul. "Now Saul, still breathing threats and murder against the disciples of the Lord...suddenly a light from heaven flashed around him...and Saul got up from the ground, and though his eyes were open, he could see nothing...the Lord Jesus...has sent me so that you may regain your sight and be filled with the Holy Spirit. And immediately there fell from his eyes something like scales, and he regained his sight, and he arose and was baptized." Acts 9:1-18.

God is MORE THAN ABLE to change your husband in an **instant**!! *I have seen it done countless times, with my own husband and with many other husbands!* If you say "But you don't know my husband," I would say – you don't know God!!

Turning the Heart

You will hear pastors and other Christians say that it is your husband's will to leave you, divorce you, or be with another woman. But we just learned in Scripture that it is not man's will but God's will.

It may be your husband's will to leave you, divorce you, or be with someone else. Nevertheless, **God can change his heart!**

We don't need to worry about his will. Instead we need to pray for our husbands' heart to be turned. "The king's **heart** is like channels of water in the hand of the LORD; **He turns** it wherever He wishes." Prov. 21:1.

Pray that God will give him a new heart and replace his heart of stone with a heart of flesh! "Moreover, I will give you a **new heart** and put a new spirit within you; and I will remove the heart of stone from your flesh and give you a **heart of flesh**." Ezek. 36:26.

The first step in turning your husband's heart is to find God's promises, His truths and then meet the conditions of those promises. *These are the verses that I memorized and used to turn Dan's heart back to me.*

"When man's ways are pleasing to the Lord, He makes even his enemies to be at peace with him." Prov. 16:7

"Delight yourself in the Lord and He will give you the desires of your heart." Ps. 37:4

"Commit your way to the Lord, trust also in Him and He will do it." Ps. 37:5

"Seek first the kingdom of God and His righteousness and all these things will be added unto you." Matt. 6:33

When you put God first in your life, He will begin to turn your husband's heart back to you. You need to renew your mind with the verses in this chapter to overcome the doubts of "man's will theology."

Let's look at the Scriptures that tell us how God changed the hearts of men and even kings:

"He put this in the king's heart...." Ezra 7:27-28.

"He hardened the hearts of the Egyptians...." Exodus 14:17.

"The Lord hardened Pharaoh's heart...." Exodus 10:27.

"The Lord turns the heart wherever He wishes...." Prov. 21:1.

In the book of Proverbs we learn wisdom. Proverbs 1 verses 2 through 7 lists the benefits of Proverbs.

To know wisdom.

To receive instruction.

To receive instruction in wise behavior.

Also instruction in righteousness, justice and equity.

Prudence to the naive.

To the youth knowledge.

Read Proverbs every day for wisdom! (Go to our website "Daily Devotional" for the verses to read every day.)

Husbands Who Are Unwilling

Not all husbands return home even after God turns their hearts. Many husbands, unfortunately, go against their hearts because their wives are the same women they chose to leave. Once again, God is MORE THAN ABLE to turn your husband's heart back to you. But, if you are still contentious, if kindness is not on your tongue, if you do not exhibit a gentle and quiet spirit, then once his heart turns toward you, the OLD you will cause him to harden his heart and make a mental decision rather than a heart decision!

Make sure you read and reread this book over and over again! Make sure you live in the Word. Make sure you spend hours daily with your face to the ground, seeking His face. You must be a new woman for your husband to want to follow his heart and come home! Remember, the reason your husband has left or has gotten caught by an adulteress is that your home was not built on the rock. It was divided; it was torn down by your words and your attitude – in other words, your contentiousness or arrogance.

Let's look at Proverbs and some New Testament Scriptures:

Her own hands. "The wise woman builds her house but the foolish tears (or "plucks" in the KJV) it down with **her own hands**." Prov. 14:1.

House of the proud. "The Lord will tear down the **house of the proud**." Prov. 14:1.

House divided against itself. "Any kingdom or house divided against itself is laid waste: and any city or **house divided against itself** shall not stand...." Matt. 12:25.

Yet it did not fall. "Therefore, everyone who hears these words of Mine, and acts upon them, may be compared to a wise man, who built his house upon the rock. And the rain descended, and the floods came, and the winds blew, and burst against that house; and **yet it did not fall**, for it had been founded upon the rock." Matt. 7:24-25.

Built together. "...Christ Jesus being the cornerstone, in whom the whole building, being fitted together, is growing into a holy temple in the Lord; in whom you also are being **built together** into a dwelling of God in the Spirit...." Eph. 2:21.

Let no man separate. "And He answered and said, 'Have you not read, that He who created them from the beginning made them male and female, and said, "for this cause a man shall leave his father and mother, and shall cleave to his wife; and the two shall become one flesh"? Consequently they are no longer two, but one flesh. What therefore God has joined together, **let no man separate**." Matt. 19:4-6.

God has promised to restore your husband to you. "Because of the iniquity of his unjust gain I was angry and struck him; I hid My face and was angry, And he went on turning away, in the way of his heart. I have seen his ways, but I will heal him; I will lead him and restore comfort to him and to his mourners, creating the praise of the lips. Peace, peace to him who is far and to him who is near, says the Lord, and I will heal him." Isa. 57:17-19.

"For perhaps he was for this reason parted *from you* for a while, that you should have him back forever, no longer as a slave [of sin], but more than a slave, a beloved brother, especially to me, but how much more to you, both in the flesh and in the Lord." Phlm. 15-16.

You must seek the Lord to break and change you if you ever hope to have your husband care for you again. (See *A Wise Woman Builds Her House: By a FOOL Who Tore Hers Down with Her Own Hands* for help.)

NOTHING is impossible for God!
The Lord Turns the Heart Wherever HE Wishes!

Personal commitment: to ask God to turn my husband's heart and not to fear the will of man. "Based on what I have learned in Scripture, I commit to trusting the Lord to turn my husband's heart. I dispel the lie that my husband has a free will; therefore, God will not intervene on my behalf and answer my prayers. Instead, I believe that my 'husband's will' will follow after God turns his heart back home."

Date: _____ Signed:_____

Chapter
11

For I Hate Divorce

" 'For I hate divorce,'
says the Lord, the God of Israel."
Malachi 2:16

Why are so many marriages ending in divorce? We have all heard the statistics...50% of **first** marriages end in divorce and 80% of **second** marriages end in divorce. That means that only 20% of second marriages survive! The real shame is that just as many marriages end in divorce IN the church!! Christians now accept divorce as an option! Why the onslaught of failed marriages?

"And the rain descended, and the floods came, and the winds blew, and burst against that house; and yet it did not fall, **for it had been founded upon the rock**." Matt. 7:25. Was your house built on the Rock? "And the rain descended, and the floods came, and the winds blew, and burst against that house; and it fell, and **great was its fall**." Matt. 7:27.

The Rock we need to build on is the Word of God! How many of us really knew the principles that you have read in this book thus far concerning marriage? Hos. 4:6 tells us that "we are perishing for a lack of knowledge." This was certainly true for me and I am sure it is true for you too!

So then when our marriage fails, we seek to be released from the marriage only to repeat the mistakes in the second or subsequent marriage. God hates divorce, but when we are in the midst of trouble that's what we believe will bring us relief. We even try to convince ourselves and others that divorce is what God wants for us since He wouldn't want us to suffer. (Go back to Chapter 4, "Various Trials" if you still believe that this is true.)

The Deception

When we entertain a wrong thought or idea, God tells us: "Each one is tempted when he is carried away and enticed by his **own lust**. (The definition of lust is a "longing" for what is forbidden, like longing for a divorce when God says "I hate divorce.") Then when lust has conceived, it gives birth to sin; and when sin is accomplished, it brings forth death. Do not be deceived, my beloved brethren." Jas 1:14-16. Many say that there is nothing wrong with divorce, especially in certain circumstances.

We must obey God rather than man. Everyone has his or her own opinion concerning marriage and divorce (what he or she "thinks" God tells us pertaining to marriage in His Word). But, "We must **obey God** rather than man." Acts 5:29.

He is our only hope for salvation. Don't follow what another person says. Instead, follow God; obey Him, for *He* is our only hope for salvation. Don't complicate His Word by trying to find "what you *think* He means." **He means exactly what He says!**

I am not ashamed of the gospel of Christ. Please stand by God's teachings regardless of what is popular or how many people in your church have divorced and/or remarried. "I am not ashamed of the gospel of Christ, for it is the power of God for salvation to everyone who believes." Rom. 1:16.

Please understand that if marriages are to be saved, we must stand on truth! Those second marriages that "seem" happy are in fact living in defeat, not a testimony of God's faithfulness. They continue to cause many others to suffer or live at less than God's best, especially the children who suffer the most! And they cause many to stumble who are experiencing difficulty in their marriages. It is very tempting to want to find a second husband when many profess that they found happiness in their second husband after they finally got rid of their first husband!

With gentleness correcting those who are in opposition. Please do not debate the issue of divorce. Each person is only responsible to speak, teach, and live the truth. Then the Holy Spirit will do the convicting, and the Lord will turn the heart. "But refuse foolish and

ignorant speculations, knowing that they produce quarrels."
"And the Lord's bond-servant must not be quarrelsome, but be kind to all, able to teach, patient when wronged, with **gentleness correcting** those who are in opposition, if perhaps God may grant them repentance leading to the knowledge of the truth, and they may come to their senses and escape from the snare of the devil, having been held captive by him to do his will." 2Tim. 2:23-26.

The tree is known by its fruit. We can see the "fruits" of many of those in church leadership – those who have allowed the widespread abuse of "exceptions" for divorce. We have seen that it began with the loophole of "unfaithfulness or adultery" and has led to divorce for practically any reason! It parallels what has happened with the abortion issue...rape, incest, and the health of the mother now account for less than 1% of all abortions performed! "You will know them by their **fruits.**" Matt. 7:16. "Either make the tree good, and its fruit good; or make the tree bad, and its fruit bad; for the tree is known by its fruit." Matt. 12:33. We can clearly see the bad fruit that has been produced by compromising God's Word – broken marriages and broken vows.

The Questions

Why must we understand and follow God's Law concerning marriage?

Because families are being destroyed, and without the family, the foundation on which our country stands will have been removed, and great will be our fall! We, as Christians, will be to blame. We cannot point the finger at others because God promises us as believers that if "My people who are **called by My name** will humble themselves and pray and seek My face and turn from their wicked ways, then I will hear from heaven, will forgive their sin, and will *heal* their land." 2Chron. 7:14.

Yet, Christian marriages are perishing at the same rate of destruction as those in the world. Why? "My people perish for a lack of knowledge." Hos. 4:6. Christians have been deceived, and are following the world's ways rather than God's ways.

How can we know that we are being deceived about marriage and divorce?

Turning aside to myths. Many of those who sit in the church pews don't want to hear the truth. "For the time will come when they will not endure sound doctrine; but wanting to have their ears tickled, they will accumulate for themselves teachers in accordance to their own desires and will turn away their ears from the truth, and will turn aside to myths." 2Tim 4:3-4.

We now seek worldly solutions for troubled or wounded marriages rather than seeking the Lord and His Word. "But you are a chosen generation, a royal priesthood, a holy nation, a *peculiar* people." 1Pet. 2:9. We are not a "peculiar people" if we just follow the beaten path that leads to the divorce court!

You may not do the things you please. His Word is always consistent; God's Word is opposed to the world's philosophies and sometimes difficult to understand and follow. "But a natural man does not accept the things of the Spirit of God; they are foolishness to him, and he cannot understand them, because they are spiritually appraised." 1Cor. 2:14. "But I say, walk by the Spirit, and you will not carry out the desire of the flesh...so you may not do the things that you please." Gal. 5:17.

Bad fruit. Again, we can easily see "the fruits" of all the Christian marriages that have been destroyed because they believed the lies. "You will know them by their fruits. Grapes are not gathered from thorn bushes, nor figs from thistles, are they? Even so, every good tree bears good fruit; but the bad tree bears **bad fruit**." Matt. 7:15-17.

Scriptural Facts to Stand On

Let's search more Scriptures to see how God views marriage.

Marriage is for life. We say the vows *until **death** do we part.* "Consequently they are no longer two but one flesh. What therefore God has joined together, let no man separate." Matt. 19:6. "AND THE TWO SHALL BECOME ONE FLESH; consequently they are no longer two, but one flesh." Mark 10:8.

God says that He hates divorce! Yet, some women are actually convinced that God led them to get a divorce! Some have said that God has "released me." **He says**... "For I hate divorce says the Lord." Malachi 2:16. He never changes... "Jesus Christ is the same yesterday and today, yes and forever." Heb. 13:8.

You are not the exception: "I most certainly understand that God is not One to show partiality." Acts 10:34.

Remarriage is not an "option" – the Bible says it's "adultery"!
"...**but I say** [Jesus Himself said] to you that everyone who divorces his wife, except for the cause of unchastity, makes her commit adultery; and whoever marries a divorced woman **commits adultery**." Matt. 5:32.

"And I say to you, whoever **divorces his** *wife*, except for immorality (fornication, KJV), and marries another woman **commits adultery.**" Matt. 19:9.

Commits adultery. "And **He** [Jesus again] said to them, 'Whoever **divorces his** *wife* and marries another woman **commits adultery** against her....'" Mark 10:11. "Everyone who **divorces his** *wife* and marries another **commits adultery;** and he who marries one who is divorced from a husband **commits adultery.**" Luke 16:18.

If her husband dies. "So then if, while her husband is living, she is joined to another man, *she* **shall be called an adulteress**; but **if her husband dies**, she is free from the law, so that she is not an adulteress, though she is joined to another man." Rom. 7:3.

Lacking sense. "The one who commits adultery with a woman is **lacking sense**; he who would destroy himself does it." Prov. 6:32. "If there is a man who commits adultery with another man's wife, one who commits adultery with his friend's wife, the adulterer and the adulteress shall surely be put to death." Lev. 20:10.

What about the "exception" clause?

Again, very few divorces in the church are for the reason of adultery, even if that were the correct "exception." Actually, in each Biblical reference, the words "adultery" and "fornication" or "moral impurity" are used **interchangeably** as though they were the same words – but they are not! The word "adultery" (Strong's Concordance in the Greek or original language is 3429 *Moichao*) means *after* marriage. The word "fornication" (4202) means *before* marriage. These are two separate sins and should not be confused.

With this information, we could rewrite the verse in Matthew with the correct translation to say: "...**but I** [Jesus] **say** that everyone who divorces his wife, makes her commit adultery; and whoever marries a divorced woman **commits adultery.**" Only when a **woman** was found *on or before* her wedding day not to be a virgin, only then could the husband divorce his wife. And again, Moses only allowed men to divorce: "Because of your hardness of heart, Moses permitted you to divorce your wives; but from the beginning it has not been this way."

In other words, NO, you cannot divorce your husband for any reason.

Be careful when you say that "God told you"! "Behold, I am against those who use their tongues and declare 'The Lord declares.' Behold, I am against those who have prophesied false dreams, declares the Lord, and related them and led my people astray by their falsehoods and reckless boasting." Jer. 23:31-32. "For I **hate** divorce, says the Lord." Malachi 2:16. God never tells us to go against His Word! He never changes! Never!!

You also must be very careful what you say about divorce or remarriage since it could lead another person to stumble and divorce or remarry: "Woe to the world because of its stumbling blocks! For it is inevitable that stumbling blocks come; but woe to that man through whom the stumbling block comes!...It is better for him that a heavy millstone be hung around his neck, and that he be drowned in the depth of the sea." Matt. 18:7, 6.

Many have been deceived. If you believe that God wants the divorce, you have been deceived. "And no wonder, for even Satan disguises himself as an angel of light." 2Cor. 11:14.

Flesh reaps corruption. "For the one who sows to his own flesh shall from the flesh reap corruption, but the one who sows to the Spirit shall from the Spirit reap eternal life." Gal. 6:8. Check to see how "driven" you are before you go step out in faith. Fleshly desires feel good to the flesh; if you have an urgency behind it, you need no grace to carry it out. "For the flesh sets its desire against the Spirit, and the Spirit against the flesh; for these are in opposition to one another, so that you may not do the things that you please." Gal. 5:17.

God and only God! What knowledge has been gained from seeing so many broken and troubled marriages? God and only God can save and keep a marriage together! By your obedience to His Word!! But you have to know His Word before you can begin to obey it. "My people perish for a lack of knowledge." Hosea 4:6. That's why you MUST read this over and over and over again! That's why you must meditate on His Word. That's why you must feed on His Word not just every day, but all day long!

Let us make a personal commitment to

REMAIN MARRIED

and encourage all we meet or talk to to do the same.

Personal commitment: to remain married and encourage others to do the same. "Based on what I have learned from God's Word, I recommit myself to my marriage. I will humble myself when necessary and take all steps as a 'peacemaker' in my marriage. I will not cover my transgressions nor cause another to stumble. I will devote my lips to spreading God's Truth on marriage in a gentle and quiet manner."

Date: _____ Signed:_____

We have put together "Restoration Fellowship" to help women find the help and support they need. Find an Encouragement Partner to meet with over the internet, or face-to-face. We pair women up with other women who are in similar situations. If your husband is still living in the home or you are separated or divorced or if your husband has remarried and you have been called to live a life of singleness, you will find comfort, support and understanding with your Encouragement Partner.

Chapter

12

Asking God

*"But if any of you lacks wisdom,
let him ask of God,
who gives to all men generously
and without reproach,
and it will be given to him."*
James 1:5

**What if my husband is unfaithful and commits adultery, then am I
allowed to divorce him?**

No! His Word says that a *husband* could divorce for the reason of
fornication only (which is intercourse prior to marriage) if the
woman was defiled, not the other way around. This exception refers
to the time of betrothal. Fornication and adultery are not the same
sin. If they were, these sins would not be stated *twice* in the same
Scripture verse: "...neither **fornicators**, idolaters, nor **adulterers**...."
1Cor. 6:9.

Divorce her secretly. Divorce for the cause of fornication was
allowed during the betrothal time, as in the case of Mary and Joseph.
The terms fiancé and engagement were not used during this period
of history. The term "husband" was used because Joseph had
already committed to being Mary's husband. "And Joseph, her
husband...desired to **divorce her secretly**." Matt. 1:19. This was
prior to their marriage because divorce was allowed for the case of
fornication only.

Betrothed. The previous verse explains that the "divorce" was to
take place **before** the marriage! "...Mary had been **betrothed** to
Joseph, **before** they came together she was found to be with
child...." Matt. 1:18. The latest a divorce could take place was

immediately after the wedding night, if the WOMAN (not the man) was found not to be a virgin. **Again, there is no Scripture that allows a woman to divorce her husband!**

Can anyone then ever remarry?

"A wife is bound as long as her husband lives; but if her husband is dead, **she is free to be married** to whom she wishes, only in the Lord." 1Cor. 7:39. For those women who are widowed, it is important to know that when the real "Mr. Right" comes along he too will be widowed or will never have been married. Remember, Satan usually brings his best first, but the Lord makes you wait and then brings His best! "Wait for the Lord, and keep His way." Ps. 37:34.

What if I am already in a second (or third) marriage?

First, you must ask God's forgiveness, whether you were married before you were saved or not. You can't be effective in your Christian walk if you can't admit past sins. "He who covers his transgressions shall not prosper." Prov. 28:13. "If we say that we have no sin, we are deceiving ourselves, and the truth is not in us. If we confess our sins, He is **faithful** and **righteous** to **forgive us our sins** and to cleanse us from **all** unrighteousness." 1John 1:8-9.

Time to repent. "And *I gave her time to repent;* and she does not want to repent of her immorality. Behold, I will cast her upon a bed of sickness, and those who commit adultery with her into great tribulation, unless they repent of her deeds." Rev. 2:2. "Therefore, confess your sins to one another, and pray for one another, so that you may be healed. The effective prayer of a righteous man can accomplish much." Jas. 5:16.

Should I restore this marriage or go back to my first husband?

His will. After you confess your sin of getting ahead of God by remarrying or marrying someone who was already married, you must lay *your* **will** aside and ask your Heavenly Father for *His* **will** concerning your present marriage. Does the Lord want you to continue to seek restoration for this marriage that is falling apart? Many women have faced this difficult task, but God is ALWAYS faithful and He will guide you if you seek Him. Pray for God's direction. "The thief comes only to steal, and kill, and destroy; I came that they might have life, and might have it abundantly." John 10:10.

What about the verse in Deuteronomy or covenant marriages?

"When a man takes a wife and marries her, and it happens that she finds no favor in his eyes because he has found some indecency in her, and he writes her a certificate of divorce and puts it in her hand and sends her out from his house, and she leaves his house and goes and becomes another man's wife, and if the latter husband turns against her and writes her a certificate of divorce and puts it in her hand and sends her out of his house, or if the latter husband dies who took her to be his wife, then her former husband who sent her away is not allowed to take her again to be his wife, since she has been defiled; for that is an abomination before the LORD, and you shall not bring sin on the land which the LORD your God gives you as an inheritance." Deut. 24:1-4.

As you can see, this passage tells a woman not to go back to her first husband. That is why we do not encourage women to think that because their second marriages are in trouble they should go back to their first husbands. Those who hold to "covenant" marriages get around this by believing that God doesn't recognize second marriages, but only first marriages. However, nowhere is this stated clearly in Scripture, and this passage contradicts this "covenant" theology. (We will discuss covenant marriages in more depth later in this section.)

Secondly, this passage specifically says that it is the woman who remarries and it speaks of *her* defilement. In a day and age when we are "blending" roles and the sexes are seen as the same, it may be hard for you to grasp, but the defilement is in the woman, not the man. This is confirmed in many verses:

"And I gave *her* time to repent; and she does not want to repent of *her* **immorality**. Behold, I will cast her upon a bed of sickness, and those who commit adultery *with* **her** into great tribulation, unless they repent of **her** deeds." Rev. 2:21-2.

This verse tells us that the punishment and sin were different for the man and woman, since it was HER immorality and HER deeds. If you want to check further, all through Leviticus you will see the protection or punishment for the defilement of the woman only.

If you have remained unmarried and undefiled then this verse really would not apply to you. However, for those who have become defiled, God sent His Son for the forgiveness of ALL sins. His blood covers YOUR defilement as well. We are no longer under the law, but live under grace when we accept the gift of salvation. God may want to restore your first marriage, or your second marriage or maybe He would rather you live a life of singleness, which some women panic at the thought. God has an abundant life for you, but only as you desire His will will you find it. If you continue to seek your own will, wanting your first marriage or your current marriage or a new marriage, you will continually live in misery and defeat. Seek Him and His will for you. "'For I know the plans that I have for you,' declares the LORD, 'plans for welfare and not for calamity to give you a future and a hope." Jer. 29:11.

An adulterous foundation. Is your present marriage a result of an adulterous relationship? Were you or was your husband married to someone else? Is that former spouse presently unmarried? If you answered yes to all three of these questions, it may be that the Lord may want you to help restore your previous marriage.

Remain single. Has your husband remarried? Then at this time, you are being called to *remain single* and not seek restoration for your marriage. If you believed wholeheartedly that you were "called" to stand for your marriage, I believe that you were correct. However, if your husband remarried, then it amy be that you tried to attain it in the flesh. You did not Biblically let him go. (For more on how and why we must let go, see Chapter 8, "Won Without a Word.")

"For the one who sows to his own flesh shall from the flesh reap corruption, but the one who sows to the Spirit shall from the Spirit reap eternal life." Gal. 6:8. You undoubtedly pursued your husband rather than Biblically letting him go (Ps. 1:1, 1Cor. 7:15). Now you must remain single and wait for your husband's present marriage to end in divorce. "...let her remain unmarried, or else be reconciled to her husband..." 1Cor. 7:11.

The truth about so-called "covenant marriages" is that God DOES recognize second marriages. In addition, the "covenant" doctrine encourages those who are in second marriages to go back to their first husbands. These doctrines contradict the verses in Deut. 24:1-4 that we opened this question with.

These verses prove that God does recognize a divorce and a remarriage because if this woman had not been remarried, she would have been in adultery, which would have resulted in her being stoned to death. These verses also prove that to encourage a woman to return to a former spouse is to encourage an abomination before the Lord. Our ministry does not encourage restoration to a former spouse, but we have seen the Lord do it. There are those who have had first marriages restored.

Covenant Marriage. The term "covenant marriage" was coined from Mal. 2:14: "Yet you say, 'For what reason?' Because the Lord has been a witness between you and the wife of your youth, against whom you have dealt treacherously, though she is your companion and your wife by covenant." It does not say that it is a first marriage or that a first marriage is all that the Lord will recognize. We cannot read into a verse what we WANT it to say. "For the time will come when they will not endure sound doctrine; but *wanting* to have their ears tickled, they will accumulate for themselves teachers in accordance to their own desires; and will turn away their ears from the truth, and will turn aside to myths." 2Tim. 4:3-4. Only the truth will set us free.

Ignoring or minimizing the power of Christ's shed blood. When you believe that God will NOT forgive a second or subsequent marriage, but sees it only as ongoing adultery, you are saying that Jesus' blood is unable to cover the sin of adultery caused by divorcing and remarrying.

But this verse tells us differently: "Or do you not know that the unrighteous shall not inherit the kingdom of God? Do not be deceived; neither fornicators, nor idolaters, nor **adulterers**...shall inherit the kingdom of God. And such **WERE some of you**; but you were washed, but you were sanctified, but you were justified in the name of the Lord Jesus Christ, and in the Spirit of our God." 1Cor. 6:9. Hallelujah! God can and does forgive adultery, any and all adultery! "And Jesus said, 'Neither do I condemn you; go your way. From now on sin no more.' " John 8:11.

Spiritual pride. Have you looked at others who are not in "covenant" marriages, who are in second or subsequent marriages, as sinners? When you believe that your husband's marriage is invalid, due to your belief that he is still *your* husband, then you elevate yourself above others, which is pride. "The Pharisee stood and was praying thus to himself, 'God, I thank Thee that I am not like other people: swindlers, unjust, adulterers, or even like this tax-gatherer. I fast twice a....'" Luke 18:11-13. The Pharisees whom Jesus always spoke against, thought that Jesus and his apostles were sinners because of their interpretation of the laws and adherence to them. The Pharisee would speak against all sinners harshly and critically out of his hardened heart.

Are you convinced that the other woman that your husband is living with or is now married to is still yours? Even in our country "possession" is more powerful than titles or deeds after enough time has passed. Whether or not my husband was living with ME is what I cared about. It's like a person whose car has been stolen. They pride themselves that they still have the title to the car, but who cares if they have the title when someone else has their car!

I was not interested in signing my husband's name to the letters I sent out or on Christmas cards. I was not content to wear my wedding rings when there was another woman he preferred to be with. I could not watch my husband divorce and remarry someone else while I stood by with other "standers."

I was determined to have my husband back home with me and my children. My husband came home to me, not because I held the title to our marriage, but because I did everything that you have read or will read in this book! I was different through my brokenness and through His ability to transform me.

Remain unmarried. Is God calling you to remain unmarried, at least for a time? It is a GOOD thing to remain unmarried. When Dan was just about to come home, I had the strongest desire to remain unmarried. It wasn't because I no longer wanted him home and my marriage restored, but because I had found that not having a husband to please let me concentrate on pleasing my Lord and Savior! "But I say to the unmarried and to widows that it is good for them if they remain even as I." 1Cor. 7:8.

"And the woman who is unmarried, and the virgin, is concerned about the things of the Lord, that she may be holy both in body and spirit; but one who is married is concerned about the things of the world, how she may please her husband. And this I say for your own benefit; not to put a restraint upon you, but to promote what is seemly, and to secure UNDISTRACTED devotion to the Lord." 1Cor. 7:34-35.

Could *you* be content to remain unmarried? If you could not, then you must take a hard look to see who is really first in your life.

Most of the women I have ministered to, who are still "standing" after a remarriage has occurred, are more obsessed with their former husbands than those whose husbands have not remarried. It has become idolatry in most cases. Getting their husbands back seems to be the most important goal in their lives! Whether your husband is remarried or not, your most important goal MUST BE a deep relationship with your Lord and Savior. He must be first in your life. If not now, WHEN?

Has your pursuit to restore your marriage caused you to stumble?

Has it caused you to become spiritually arrogant? Has it become idolatry? Have you become unfruitful in your Christian walk due to your longing for your spouse or marriage or for your former spouse and former marriage?

Trust Him. If you want the abundant life God has for you as one of His children, you must trust Him with your life. God wants to give you an abundant life, not a counterfeit. If you choose to try and do this yourself, it is in vain. Ps. 127:1 says, "Unless the Lord builds the house, they labor in vain who build it...." Please, pray from your heart, "Father, if Thou art willing, remove this cup from Me; yet **not** *My will*, but **Thine** be done." Luke 22:42.

Contentment. I KNEW that if God allowed Dan to marry the other woman (as Dan told me he was going to do), then God was telling me to stay on *this* side of the Jordan and be content. The closer my relationship with the Lord became the more this possibility didn't frighten me. Actually near the very end just before God restored my marriage, it sounded wonderful and exciting!

If you are having trouble dealing with the concept of contentment, then I would encourage you to see our Q & A video "Avoiding and Dealing with Remarriage." No matter what your present situation, it will bless you and bring you hope. Here is a testimony from a woman who has a restored marriage: *"As I watched the video I got more excited and more excited. It was truly anointed. Anyone who wants a miracle in their life should apply the concepts in this video!"*

Can adultery be forgiven?

Yes. Jesus said to the woman caught in adultery: "Did no one condemn you? ... Neither do I condemn you; go your way. From now on sin no more." John 8:10-11. Actually, not only is **adultery** NOT grounds for divorce, it is **grounds for forgiveness** as Christ showed in John 8:10 above.

We also have an example in Hosea of a spouse forgiving adultery in Hos. 3:1. "Then the Lord said to me, 'Go again, love a woman who is loved by her husband, yet an adulteress.' " Then in 1Cor. 6:9-11, when God refers to adulterers and fornicators, He says: "And such **were** some of you; but you were washed, but you were sanctified, but you were justified in the name of the Lord Jesus Christ, and in the Spirit of our God." We are washed in His blood of forgiveness.

Yet, many pastors say that adultery is grounds for divorce. "You have heard that it was said, 'You shall not commit adultery'; but I say to you that everyone who *looks* on a woman to lust for her has committed adultery with her already in his heart." Matt. 5:27-28. If it is true that adultery is grounds for divorce, then most married women could divorce their husbands since most men have lusted over pictures of women on television or in magazines!

If you have committed adultery, you must confess your sin to your husband if he is unaware of your unfaithfulness. "He who conceals his transgressions will not prosper, but he who confesses and forsakes them will find compassion." Prov. 28:13.

Isn't remarriage okay if it's under the right circumstances?

So many churches and pastors say that divorce is right in some situations, but this verse says, "Whoever then annuls one of the least of these commandments, and so teaches others, shall be called least in the kingdom of heaven; but whoever keeps and teaches them, he shall be called great in the kingdom of heaven." Matt. 5:19.

How can I be sure that what **this** book says is right and what many of the churches are saying is wrong? "Beware of the false prophets, who come to you in sheep's clothing, but inwardly are ravenous wolves. Many will say to Me on that day, 'Lord, Lord, did we not prophesy in Your name, and in Your name cast out demons, and in Your name perform many miracles?' And then I will declare to them, ' I never knew you; Depart from Me, you who practice lawlessness.' " Matt. 7:15-23. Aren't many of the marriages in your church crumbling and the families dissolving? These are the bad fruits.

Many pastors feel a "deep down" conviction about marriage, but don't want to "offend" anyone, especially all those "church members" who are in their second and third marriages. "Friendship with the world is hostility toward God. Therefore whoever wishes to be a friend of the world makes himself an enemy of God." Jas. 4:4.

Ears tickled. If a pastor or church takes a stand against divorce and remarriage, they are labeled legalistic or judgmental. And those who want to "do their own thing" will go to another church to hear what they want to hear (to have their ears tickled).

"For the time will come when they will not endure sound doctrine; but wanting to have their **ears tickled**, they will accumulate for themselves teachers in accordance to their own desires; and will turn away from the truth, and will turn aside to myths." 2Tim. 4:3-4.

Since I'm already divorced or single again, couldn't I remarry or at least date and then ask God to forgive me?

First of all, **you are not single.** Only someone who has *never* been married (or who is a widow) is single. "So then if, while her husband is living, she is joined to another man, **she shall be called an adulteress**; but if her husband dies, she is free from the law, so that she is not an adulteress, though she is joined to another man." Rom. 7:3.

Secondly, you will reap what you have sown. "Do not be deceived, God is not mocked; for whatever a man sows, this he will reap also." Gal. 6:7. You are willfully entering into sin. "Therefore to one who knows the right thing to do and does not do it, to him it is sin." Jas. 4:17.

A terrifying thing. You'll set yourself up for God's vengeance. "For if we go on sinning willfully after receiving the knowledge of the truth, there no longer remains a sacrifice for sins. How much more **severe a punishment** do you think he will deserve who has trampled under foot the Son of God. Vengeance is mine, I will repay. The Lord will judge His people. *It is a terrifying thing to fall into the hands of the living God.*" Heb. 10:26-31.

Note: In the last few months, the Lord has been flooding me with much knowledge about those who have "known the truth" and yet ignored it in order to do "**as they pleased.**" Some of the most horrible, abominable, and heart-wrenching testimonies I have ever heard have just recently been shared with me.

Ladies, God will not be mocked. You will not benefit from ignoring God's Word, nor by trading obedience for a "better marriage" (or relationship) with someone new.

If You Love Me

In closing, "If anyone advocates a different doctrine and does not agree with sound words, those of our Lord Jesus Christ, and with the doctrine conforming to godliness, he is conceited and understands nothing; but has a morbid interest in controversial questions and disputes about words, out of which arise envy, strife, abusive language, evil suspicions, and constant friction between men of truth." 1Tim. 6:3-5.

"If you love Me, you will keep My commandments." John 14:15. If you say you believe God, **then obey Him**. "Why do you call me

Lord and not do what I say?" Luke 6:46. If you have decided to ask Jesus for your salvation but are not following His teachings, then He is not your Lord and Master. If He *is* your Lord, then be sure that you act like it. Obey Him!

Let us make a personal commitment to
SEEK THE LORD
and encourage all others to do the same!

Personal commitment: to seek the Lord as to whether I am to restore my present marriage. "Based on what I have learned from God's Word, I commit to ask God whether or not I am to restore this marriage. I will lay aside my will, wanting only His will since He is my Lord. I will never judge anyone who is in a second or subsequent marriage, but acknowledge that the blood of Jesus is able to cover the sin of adultery."

Date: _____ Signed:_____

Testimony: Restored After Husband Remarried

A woman from California wrote to me about restoring her marriage. Things were progressing very nicely and both she and I were hopeful that her marriage would soon be restored. However, one day she heard through a friend that her husband had married the other woman. Despondent, she wrote to me, "What now?"

I shared with her much of what you have just read in this chapter on remarriage. She wrote back and thanked me. She said that once she became content with God's apparent will for her life, and gave up her will for His, she was now at peace and content to live a single life, never to marry (she was in her early thirties).

Within the year, she wrote back that her former husband recently contacted her. He said that he realized that he had made the biggest mistake of his life! He had already separated from the new wife and was filing for divorce. He wanted to know if she would consider dating him again or if she would only consider it after he was legally divorced. He told her that it was his intent to marry her again if she would have him!

I have shared the principle of COMPLETELY letting go of a husband who has remarried with a strong and bold statement with several other women. All of them rejected this counsel, except this ONE woman who now has a restored marriage! This ONE woman had never been to Covenant Keepers or heard of "covenant" marriages, a term that was coined from the one Scripture in Malachi.

In our ministry, we have never seen one man or one woman return after a remarriage, save this ONE only. But again, let me emphasize, this was the only woman who ever took the Scriptural counsel.

Once left alone, her former husband was able to feel the full impact of his wrong decision to marry the other woman. He had not seen or heard from his former wife during this time, but had to track her down to find her (they had no children). I say this to those who are afraid to let go, for fear that God is unable to bring a person back.

Prayerfully consider becoming a member of our Restoration Fellowship to help you to see YOUR marriage through to restoration. You can find out about the many benefits of becoming a member on our website.

Chapter

13
Wonderful Counselor

"And His name will be called
Wonderful Counselor,
Mighty God,
Eternal Father,
Prince of Peace."
Isaiah 9:6

My husband is filing for divorce; what should I do?

How do I find someone to defend me?

How can I protect myself and especially my children?

Many Christians, counselors and even pastors will advise you to get a good Christian lawyer to protect you and your children. However, when I was faced with this same dilemma, I looked to Scripture and went to the "Mighty Counselor."

I found in His Word that He had promised to protect and defend me! I chose Him and did what His Word told me to do. He was not only faithful, but mightier than any attorney or court could be because I put my trust in Him ALONE!

Who has known the mind of the Lord? "Oh, the depth of the riches both of the wisdom and knowledge of God! How unsearchable are His judgments and unfathomable His ways! For **who has known the mind of the Lord,** or who became His counselor?" Rom. 11:33-34. Speak to the Lord. Then **sit quietly** and **hear** from Him.

Woe to the rebellious. Egypt represents the world. " '**Woe to the rebellious** children,' declares the Lord, 'Who execute a plan, but not

Mine, and make an alliance, but not of My Spirit, in order to add sin to sin; Who proceed down to Egypt, without consulting Me, to take refuge in the safety of Pharaoh, and to seek shelter in the shadow of Egypt!' " Isa. 30:1-2.

Have you sought protection in the court system? Do you trust your attorney MORE than you do your Lord? "...Cursed is the man who trusts in mankind and makes flesh his strength." It makes your heart turn "away from the LORD." Jer. 17:5.

It shall not approach you. "And if anyone wants to sue you and take your shirt, let him have your coat also." Matt. 5:38-48. Usually we are worried that our husbands won't take care of us and that they'll take too much of what we or our children deserve. If you act like he's your enemy and fight, he'll fight back. Hasn't he in the past?

Many share "horror stories" about those who have divorced to scare you into getting a good lawyer. Just remember, "A thousand may fall at your side, and ten thousand at your right hand, but **it shall not approach you**." Ps. 91:7. Instead, "Do not be overcome by evil, but overcome evil with good." Rom. 12:21. Release your attorney and trust God ALONE to deliver and protect you.

Dare go before the unrighteous versus saints? "Does any one of you, when he has a case against his neighbor, dare to go to law before the unrighteous, and not before the saints?" 1Cor. 6:1. This is a very firm Scripture. Would we dare God? If you merely show up in court, you are standing "before the unrighteous."

In most states you would not violate the law if you didn't show up in court if you were served with divorce papers. You merely lose by default. Some make you sign a waiver that you will not appear, and in some you neither have to sign the papers nor show up. (Our *Facing Divorce* book will help you with many of your questions.)

Check it out and don't just take one person's word for it if they tell you you "have to" do anything. *I took this verse literally when I was served my divorce papers. I didn't sign the papers nor did I show up for the hearing – and God delivered me! Had I gone to an attorney or shown up in court, I would not have seen the mighty deliverance by the hand of God!*

We shall judge angels. "Or do you not know that the saints will judge the world? And if the world is judged by you, are you not competent to constitute the smallest law courts? Do you not know that **we shall judge angels**? How much more, matters of this life?" 1Cor. 6:2-3. God is mocking us, showing us how petty and insignificant the matters of this world are in comparison to our life with Him.

Matters of this life. "If then you have law courts **dealing with matters of this life**, do you appoint them as judges who are of no account in the church?" 1Cor. 6:4. The courts today do not follow Biblical teachings as they did when this country was founded. As a result, we have rulings and burdens placed upon believers that neither God nor our founding fathers had in mind. If you choose the courts to help you, you will choose *their* judgment over God's protection and provisions.

Before unbelievers. "I say this to your shame. Is it so, that there is not among you one wise man who will be able to decide between his brethren, but brother goes to law with brother, and that **before unbelievers**?" 1Cor. 6:5. When the church began to ignore the Biblical teachings, they also began to ignore the church's correction.

I have NEVER heard of a man who turned from his sin of adultery after being confronted by the church. Some temporarily changed, but in all cases they returned to the other woman! Don't continue to manipulate and ask your pastor to talk to your husband. Allow God to turn and soften your husband's heart.

Rather be wronged or defrauded. "Actually, then, it is already a defeat for you, that you have lawsuits with one another. Why not rather be **wronged**? Why not rather be **defrauded**? On the contrary, you yourselves wrong and defraud, and that your brethren." 1Cor. 6:7-8. God says it is better that you are wronged and defrauded (cheated or tricked).

Most women that I speak to who are in the process of divorcing are so caught up in what they'll get, how much money for support and how many possessions. If you don't allow yourself to be wronged, your husband will end up angry and bitter. If you don't allow yourself to be backed up to the Red Sea, you will never see God's power of deliverance! Remember that the "cares and riches of the world will choke the Word!" (Matt. 13:22)

We are told that Demas left Paul because the cares of the world choked the Word from him. The following verse tells us how... "And the one on whom seed was sown among the thorns, this is the man who hears the word, and the **worry** of the world and the deceitfulness of **riches** choke the word, and it becomes unfruitful." Matt. 13:22. Scripture says specifically that it was because of "worry" and because of "riches." Don't worry about or get caught up with money or possessions.

Trust that "Our God will supply all our needs," even when your papers say that he doesn't have to pay enough child support or it doesn't "look" like there will be enough money for you and your children. Many have fallen from their faith because the Word was choked out.

My divorce papers stated that I wouldn't get nearly enough to support myself and my four small children. But God softened my husband's heart because I trusted the Lord. I didn't even need to ask for more or tell him my plight. God placed in my husband's heart the desire to pay all of our bills until he came home! We hear so MANY testimonies when the husband continued to pay most if not all the bills even though it was NOT on the divorce papers when the women concentrated on the heart of her husband and followed the principles in the Facing Divorce *book.*

Because you are lukewarm. Don't get a lawyer. If you have one, dismiss him or her. Every one of the women who tried to convince others that it was all right to compromise any of the Scriptural principles that are written in this book or in *A Wise Woman*, is still living a life of singleness. Maybe this is not what you want to hear. It is not what I like to write either. But I must resist allowing my heart to govern what is written for Him or He will cease to use me.

A defeat for you. "Actually, then it is already **a defeat for you**, that you should have lawsuits with one another. Why not rather be wronged? Why not rather be defrauded?" 1Cor. 6:7. This is your answer: if you go into court with your spouse, it is already a defeat for you. You may get the money or the possessions, but you will lose your husband!

No one will see the Lord. "Pursue peace with all men, and sanctification without which **no one will see the Lord**." Heb. 12:14-15. If you wish to act as Jesus acted (who was totally innocent) remember that He "opened not His mouth in defense," 1Pet. 2:23. God can begin to work in your husband's life because you are planting seeds of life and no longer giving Satan fuel for destruction (see 1Pet. 3:1).

We want our husbands to see Jesus' ways in us. We quench the work of the Holy Spirit when we do the things we "want to" instead of what we "ought to." Do it **God's way!**

Put away. "Let all bitterness, wrath and anger and clamor and slander be **put away** with all malice." Eph. 4:31. If you have a lawyer, slander and wrath WILL take place. This is what divorce is all about. You must put it away from you. It doesn't matter if you have a "Christian" attorney or not – all "**deliverance by _man_ is in vain**"!

Deliverance by MAN is in vain. "O, give us help against the adversary, for **deliverance by man is in vain**." Ps. 108:12-13. I have heard countless accounts of all the ways that people try to deliver themselves, only to find that even though the judge gives a judgment of a certain amount of money or protection, the courts can't make your husband pay or protect you from his vengeance or physical harm!

There has been much media attention given to those who don't pay child support. You have heard stories about men who come after their wives for physical revenge — and law enforcement can't help them! Allow God to turn your husband's heart (Prov. 21:1). Your husband doesn't need stricter penalties, but a heart for you and your children. You have His promise: "When a man's ways [_your_ ways] are pleasing to the Lord, He makes even his enemies to be at peace with him." Prov. 16:7.

Take refuge in the Lord. "It is better to **take refuge in the Lord** than to trust in man." Ps. 118:8. A lawyer is no substitute for the Lord. If you think you can have both a lawyer and God's protection the following verse explains that they are opposing one another. "Cursed is the man who trusts in mankind and makes flesh his strength. Blessed is the man who trusts in the Lord and **whose trust is the Lord**." Jer. 17:5-8. You can either be blessed or cursed. You decide.

Cease striving. "**Cease striving** and know that I am God." Ps. 46:8-10. Put it in His hands. Stop wringing your hands about it; stop discussing it with everyone. Be still! If your husband has already begun divorce proceedings, and you have already humbled yourself and turned from your wicked ways, then follow these steps:

Called us to peace. Tell your husband that you do not want the divorce, but that you will not stand in his way (Ps. 1:1) and that you will NOT contest the divorce either. Tell him that you don't "blame him" for wanting to divorce you. Tell him that you will still love him (if the "hate wall" is down), no matter what he chooses to do. "Yet if the unbelieving one leaves, let him leave...but God has

called us to peace." 2Cor. 7:15.

Sweetness of speech. Again, be sure to tell your husband that you will not contest or fight him in the divorce and that you won't get a lawyer for yourself. (If you have a lawyer, tell your husband that you will dismiss him or her.) Tell your husband that you trust him and know from his past that he will be fair, and that he will do what he believes is right for you and your children. "**Sweetness of speech** adds persuasiveness." Prov. 6:24.

I hate divorce. Tell your husband that you have made so many mistakes in the past that you don't want to make any more. You hope that he will allow you NOT to sign the divorce papers. I told my husband that since our was a state of "no-fault" the divorce would go through even if I did not sign the papers. Seek the Lord for how He wants to deliver you and the words that He wants you to speak to your husband. Remember, the Lord said, "**I hate divorce**." Of course if he persists in your signing, agree to sign and then pray diligently that the Lord will stop him from pursuing you to sign. If you are not the same disagreeable woman that you were, and your husband sees a humble and meek wife, then he will not continue to press. Don't offer suggestions to try and please your husband; this is displeasing to the Lord. Seek the Lord! (See "Wives, Be Subject" under the heading "Sarah's Obedience: Submission unto Sin?" in *A Wise Woman*.)

Nothing is impossible. However, if you have participated in the divorce procedure, all is not lost. Ask the Lord's forgiveness and your husband's forgiveness also. Demonstrate your desire that you want the family together by dropping any and all legal action or protection. God will begin to heal right now: "*With God nothing is impossible*." Matt 19:26. If you have retained a lawyer, dismiss him or her immediately if you want the Best to defend you. Then pray, "Lord, there is no one besides Thee to help us in the battle between the powerful and those who have no strength; so help us, O Lord our God, for we trust in Thee, and in Thy name have come against this, O Lord, Thou art our God; let not man prevail against Thee." 2Chron. 14:11.

Harder to be won. If you have already been through a divorce, bitterness and resentment and extreme anger are probably what your husband feels toward you now. Pray that God will forgive your transgressions and blot out the bad memories he has (Ps. 9:5) and replace them with good thoughts. Pray harder and be sweeter (again, sweetness of speech adds persuasiveness) at every opportunity that you may have with your husband to win him back. Remember, "A brother offended is **harder to be won** than a strong city, and contentions are like the bars of a castle." Prov. 18:19. (See Chapter 8, "Won Without a Word.")

Then I could bear it. God does understand what you are going through. Read some of Ps. 55; He's speaking directly to you. Beginning in verse 6, "Oh that I had wings like a dove! I would fly away and be at rest. Behold, I would wander far away, I would lodge in the wilderness. I would hasten to my place of refuge, from the stormy wind and tempest." Vs. 12-14: "For it is not an enemy who reproaches me, **then I could bear it**; nor is it one who hates me who exalted himself against me, then I could hide myself from him. But it is you, a man my equal, my companion and my familiar friend, we who had sweet fellowship together...."

Steal, and kill, and destroy. If you have "flown away" go back home. Satan is in his glory because he has again managed to divide and conquer! Take back the ground that he stole from you; he is a thief! "The thief comes only to **steal, and kill, and destroy**; I came that they might have life, and might have it abundantly." John 10:10. Give God the victory and the testimony by turning this around for **His** glory! Instead of throwing away "your cross" (your troubled marriage), pick it up again and follow Him!

Take up his cross daily. "And He was saying to them all, 'If anyone wishes to come after Me, let him deny himself, and **take up his cross daily**, and follow Me.' " Luke 9:23. Be sure that your cross isn't heavier than He has designed for you; take off all your lack of forgiveness and bitterness. It's a heavy weight to carry and, eventually, you won't be able to continue to carry it. You may not even be able to lift it up now, to begin to follow Him.

Take off any "works of the flesh." The flesh will wear you out and break you down. Let go and let God restore. Use this time to fall in love with the Lord! If your cross feels too heavy to bear, there are burdens on your cross that *you* have put there. He does not lie and He has promised that He wouldn't give us more than we could bear!

There is no one besides Thee. Now let us together pray as Asa prayed in 2Chron. 14:11: "Lord, **there is no one besides Thee** to help in the battle between the powerful and those who have no strength; so help us, O Lord our God, for we trust in Thee, and in Thy name have come against this multitude. O Lord, thou art our God; let not man prevail against Thee."

Below are a few short testimonies from those who have chosen to follow the ways of the world or the ways of God:

Testimony: A woman came into class for the first time only a week before she was to take the "evidence" of her husband's infidelity to her attorney. The attorney said that if she could show this to the judge, he could get her more money. The lesson that night was "Wonderful Counselor." Without saying a word in class, she went home and threw the shoe box full of "evidence" into the trash. Since then, her husband has continued to pay her bills though he married another. She is still praying and trusting God.

Testimony: A young woman believed God when she read that "He is our Provider." When she read the divorce papers, which stated that she was barely going to get enough to pay the small rent payment for herself and her children, she made up her mind to continue to trust God. Then she acted on her faith. She told her husband that she trusted him and that she was sure that he would help take care of them as he had done so faithfully in the past. He did continue to pay **all** their bills and even gave her spending money from time to time out of his girlfriend's savings! The other woman and the attorney tried to falsify the divorce papers, but they were not able to succeed because God had turned her husband's heart. The divorce did go through, but shortly thereafter, they were remarried.

Testimony: A woman tearfully contacted us whose husband had filed for divorce. She said that she also had a friend who had filed. She said that she was so sympathetic that she failed to share with her friend about her own troubled marriage and that she was trusting God to help her.

A few weeks later she heard a shocking report on the news: her friend's husband was so distraught about the divorce that he planned to kill his wife before he would let her leave. Yet the net which he had hidden caught his own foot; he died in the fire that also destroyed their entire house.

Testimony: An older woman came to Restore Ministries after her divorce was final (though a friend had begged her for months to come!). She shared with others the devastating effects of fighting it out in court. She did receive "all that she deserved": the house, a new car and alimony. Yet she now has a former husband who will have nothing to do with her. He has thousands of dollars worth of bitterness that the court made him pay to her and to her divorce lawyer.

Testimony: A woman came to a prayer group (not Restore Ministries) asking that they pray for her upcoming divorce. They prayed that God would have the judge provide well for her and her children. God answered that prayer and the court awarded her an ample amount of money in the divorce. Only a few months later she was asking for prayer again since her husband had not paid her a dime! Again they prayed for the court to be firm with her husband. The judgment again was in her favor.

Only weeks later she asked that the prayer group pray that the police would "find him" and bring him back for "justice"! He had fled to another state to avoid paying. At this point the police threw him into jail. That prayer group failed to really trust God for her protection, for Him to turn her husband's heart and have him "want" to provide for his family. "And *my* **God** shall supply all your needs according to His riches in glory in Christ Jesus." Phil. 4:19. Only God's way will bring "victory."

Don't follow the world's way; trust only in Him. I promise you that He will never let you down. Only as you compromise or look to the flesh for strength and protection will things go awry. Still, it may take going through the fire of endurance (*with* Him) to reach the victory He has waiting for you. Will you pick up your cross and follow Him?

How much faith do you have? Enough to take the step to allow the Lord to fight for you without a lawyer? My beloved sister in Christ, release your attorney, and take the hand of Jesus.

Personal commitment: to trust God alone. "Based on what I have learned in Scripture, I commit to trusting the Lord to fight for me in this battle. I will release my attorney (if I have one) and I will not show up in court (unless I will be in contempt)."

Date: _____ Signed:_____

If you still are not convicted to release your attorney, drop ANY and all legal dealings that you instigated against your husband, and seek to not appear in court, then I beg you to REREAD this entire chapter! PLEASE order our book **Facing Divorce** *if you have any reservations about dropping all legal action with your husband. It is filled with those who trusted the Lord to release their attorney and their marriage was restored! My only desire is to see your marriage restored. Is it your only desire too?*

Chapter

14

First to Throw a Stone

*"He who is without sin among you,
let him be the first to
throw a stone."*
John 8:7

Adultery
Grounds for Forgiveness

Should adultery ever be forgiven? What did Jesus do? Jesus said to the woman caught in adultery, "Did no one condemn you? ...Neither do I condemn you; go your way. From now on, sin no more." John 8:10-11. Have you condemned your husband?

Are you without sin, that you should cast the first stone at your husband? Jesus also said to the people who wanted this adulterous woman punished, "He who is without sin among you, cast the first stone." John 8:7. Are you without sin, that you should cast the first stone at your husband? The truth is, "If we say that we have no sin, we are deceiving ourselves, and the truth is not in us." 1John 1:8.

But I never did anything that sinful! Let me show you that God groups your sins along with your husband's. This is how God sees sin: "Now the deeds of the flesh are evident, which are: (his?) immorality, impurity, sensuality...drunkenness, carousing, (now yours?) strife, jealousy, outbursts of anger, disputes, dissensions, envying." Gal. 5:19-20.

And if I don't forgive him? What are the grave consequences of unforgiveness? "But if you do not forgive men for their transgressions, your heavenly Father will not forgive your transgression." Matt. 6:15.

When God refers to adulterers and fornicators, He says, "And such *were* some of you; but you were washed, but you were **sanctified**, but you were justified in the name of the Lord Jesus Christ and in the spirit of our God." 1Cor. 6:9-11. "For the unbelieving husband is **sanctified** through his wife." 1Cor. 7:14. Since you and your husband are one flesh, we at Restore Ministries suggest that you draw closer to God, allowing Him to transform you more into His image. Something amazing will begin happening to your husband since you are one flesh – He will become sanctified! However, as long as you stay in sin, you will both stay unsanctified.

But adultery has happened before! Let us remember what Jesus said to us when asked how often we are to forgive someone. "If he sins against you seven times a day, and returns to you seven times, saying 'I repent,' forgive him seven times seventy." Luke 17:1-4. (See Chapter 9, "A Gentle and Quiet Spirit" on the subject of "Tough Love.") Also, see below for why it continues.

But he hasn't repented! As Jesus hung on the cross for *your* sins, He cried out, "Father forgive them, for they know not what they do." Luke 23:34. (Again, see Chapter 9, "A Gentle and Quiet Spirit" on "Forgiveness.")

"Don't be overcome with evil, but overcome evil with good." God specifically asked His prophet Hosea to remarry his wife Gomer, even after she was blatantly unfaithful to him. Hosea 2:2 "For she is not my wife, and I am not her husband...." vs. 7 "Then she will say, 'I will go back to my first husband, for it was better for me then than now.' " vs. 3:1 "Then the Lord said to me (Hosea), 'Go again, love a woman who is loved by her husband, yet an adulteress.' " God used the story of Hosea and Gomer to show His commitment to His own bride, the church (see the book of Hosea). And also Luke 15: the older son said to his father "...this son of yours came, who devoured your wealth with harlots, you killed the fatted calf for him." Then the father said to his older son, "But we had to be merry and rejoice, for this brother of yours was dead and has begun to live, and was lost and has been found." What will your husband find when he calls or comes by? The fatted calf, your robe and a ring or will he be met with judgment?

Can I ever trust him again? God said to trust **Him**; you will then be blessed with a faithful husband. "Cursed is the man who trusts mankind and makes flesh his strength...Blessed is the man who trusts in the Lord and whose trust is the Lord." Jer. 17:5-7. People always ask me how I can trust my husband. I answer by saying, "I don't – I trust the Lord!" It is the Lord who made my husband faithful to me and He will keep him faithful. Glory to God!

How can I help my husband? Help him by praying... "Keep watching and praying, that you may not come into temptation; the spirit is willing, but the flesh is weak." Mark 14:38. Every woman who *allowed* God to turn her husband's heart testifies that God removed the wandering eyes and unfaithfulness. (These are women whose husbands have been back home for years!) God may bring other tests into our lives, to be sure, but not adultery. Nevertheless, when God heals, **it is finished!** But remember, if you sow the flesh you will reap the flesh. Some women coerce or entice their husbands to return home. Learn to wait. When it is the blessing of the Lord, He will add no sorrow to it! (Prov. 10:22)

What to do or not do
if your husband is in adultery

The adulteress flatters; we are instead to edify. Prov. 29:5 "A man who flatters his neighbor is spreading a net for his steps." Eph. 4:29. "Let no unwholesome word proceed out of your mouth, but only such a word as is good for edification." The difference between flattering and edifying is the heart. When someone flatters, the heart or motivation is to "get something." The motivation of one who edifies or builds up, is to give something – expecting nothing in return. Two women can be saying the same thing, yet the difference is in their hearts. What kind of heart do you have? Do you whine and complain to others about what your husband hasn't done in return for your kindness and forgiveness? Whether he hears your whining is not important. God hears it and is looking at your heart.

God may bring on His wrath; don't you do it! "Therefore consider the members of your earthly body as dead to immorality, impurity, passion, evil desire, and greed, which amounts to idolatry. For on account of these things the wrath of God will come." Col. 3:5-6. "For we know Him who said, 'Vengeance is mine, I will repay, and again, the Lord will judge His people. It is a terrifying thing to fall into the hands of the living God.' " Heb. 10:30-31. If you haven't forgiven your husband you may be joyful when the "wrath from God" begins. However, God warns us: "Do not rejoice when your enemy falls, and do not let your heart be glad when he stumbles; lest the Lord see it and be displeased, and He turn away His anger from him." Prov. 24:18.

Don't be deceived – you don't need to look into what your husband is doing. "For nothing is hidden that shall not become evident, nor anything secret that shall not be known and come to light." Luke 8:17. They have been hidden from you by God to protect you. Those who thwart God's protection by spying or investigating are **tragic**; please don't make the same mistake! "For it is disgraceful **even to speak** of the things which are done by them in secret." Eph. 5:12. And ladies, stop talking about your husband's sinful life. It does not glorify God. Only the adversary is delighted that you are so willing to speak for him!

What Can We Learn from Scripture About the Adulterer and the Adulteress?

It's flattery that pulls a man into adultery. "For the **lips** of an adulteress drip honey and *smoother than oil* is her **speech**; but in the end she is bitter as wormwood, sharp as a two-edged sword. Her feet go down to death, her steps lay hold of Sheol. She does not ponder the path of life; *her ways are unstable, she does not know it.*" Prov. 5:3-6. While you were busy tearing him down, the OW was building him up. While you were disagreeing, she was agreeing. Has it changed?

She uses her flattery to pull him into adultery and into spiritual death. "With her many persuasions *she* entices *him*; with her flattering lips *she* seduces *him*. **Suddenly** he follows her as an ox goes to slaughter. So he does not know it will cost him his life." Prov. 7:21-23. Many times it is quite suddenly that he follows her. Many women whose husbands have fallen into the pit of adultery have reported that they warned their husbands, yet they never heeded their wives' warnings. (See Chapter 8, "Won Without a Word" for why husbands ignore their wives' warnings.)

Once again it is her flattery that pulls a man into adultery. "That they may keep you from an adulteress, from the foreigner who **flatters** with her **words**." Prov. 7:5. When was the last time you praised your husband for anything? Encouraged him? Got excited about what he said? Is it any wonder he was starving for what the adulteress was serving – flattery?

Again it is her flattery that eventually pulls him down to suffering financially. "To keep you from the evil woman, from the **smooth tongue** of the adulteress. Do not desire her beauty in your heart, do not let her catch you with her eyelids. For on account of a harlot one is **reduced to a loaf of bread,** and an adulteress hunts for the precious life. Can a man take fire to his bosom, and his clothes not be burned? The one who commits adultery with a woman *is lacking sense*; he who would destroy himself does it. Wounds and disgrace he will find, and his reproach will not be blotted out." Prov. 6:24-33. So many women are surprised by their husbands' actions or what they say while in adultery. The Bible is clear: at this point he *is lacking sense* and is *destroying himself.*

And again God says that he will suffer financially. "He who keeps company with harlots *wastes* his **wealth.**" Prov. 29:3. There have been women who have come to me to tell me that, because her husband is so successful corporately, this will never happen to him. God's Word applies to all. Every woman who came to debate this principle later told me of her husband's financial collapse and how the adulteress wasted his wealth!

The adulteress is basically out to get the man. She is out (of the home) to do it! "A woman comes to meet him, dressed as a harlot and cunning of heart, **she is boisterous and rebellious; her feet do not remain at home.**" Prov. 7:5. Is this a description of you too? Are you boisterous? Are you rebellious? Do you spend more time away from home than in it? "For the harlot is a deep pit, and an adulterous woman is a narrow well. She lurks as a *robber*, and *increases the faithless* among man." Prov. 23:28. (Please read, "The Ways of Her Household" in *A Wise Woman Builds Her House: By a FOOL Who Tore Hers Down with Her Own Hands* for more knowledge.)

The adulteress is deceived into thinking that she has done nothing wrong. "This is the way of an adulterous woman: she eats and wipes her mouth, and says, '**I have done nothing wrong.**'" Prov. 30:20. Many women who come seeking help for their marriages respond in the same way by stating "**I have done nothing wrong.**" Have you taken the full responsibility for your marriage collapsing? Until you look directly at what you have done long and hard enough that you can no longer see your husband's sin, your marriage will not be restored.

The adulteress is an enemy of God! "You adulteresses, do you not know that friendship with the world is hostility with God? Therefore, whoever wishes to be a friend of the world makes himself **an enemy of God.**" Jas. 4:4.

God will give her time to repent and then cause great tribulation! "And I gave her time to repent; and she does not want to repent of her immorality. Behold, I will *cast her upon a bed of* **sickness**, and those who commit adultery with her into **great tribulation**, unless they repent of her deeds." Rev. 2:22. We see this so often in our ministry. All the men who stayed in adultery eventually fell into "great tribulation." This is why it is vital that when your husband is seeking relief he "knows" that there is peace in his own home. He must KNOW that the contentious woman is gone! If God hasn't brought him around, then you are not ready. God is more than able to create a situation in your husband's life to cause him to contact you. It's not God's problem or your husband's problem; it's your problem. Once there is a significant change, God will be faithful to bring him around. Until that time He is hiding you with the desire to change and mold you from the inside out.

We have also seen at least four cases when the other woman, who would not repent after a time, was stricken with a significant illness (i.e., lupus, cancer).

"And I will *kill her children* with **pestilence**; and all the churches will know that I am He who searches the minds and hearts; and I will give to each one of you according to your deeds." Rev. 2:23. In addition we know of two cases when a child died. One woman lost a child in a miscarriage to what the doctors said was a "parasite." We in Restore Ministries just heard of another case when the other woman (a professed Christian) in her boldness continued to pursue another woman's husband after many warnings. Her oldest son died of a brain tumor!

This is a spiritual battle. It must be fought and won in the Spirit. We have prayers at the end of Chapters 16 and 17, taken directly from Scripture, for you to pray to restore your marriage, specifically in the case of adultery. Please ignore and resist the temptation to fight in the flesh, either viciously or seductively. Books, talk shows and well-meaning friends may try to sway you either to administer the "tough love" approach that WILL lead to disaster or to seduce him. Neither of these is the cause or the solution to this sin. **It is a spiritual battle. It must be fought and WON in the Spirit!** However, love (as found in 1Cor. 13) is always the right response!

Seducing is very different from alluring. Kind and loving words are alluring. Forgiveness is alluring. Someone who is at peace is alluring. Don't fail to allure your husband through kindness, with loving words which speak loud and clear that you truly have forgiven him. "Therefore, behold, I will **allure** her, bring her into the wilderness, and speak kindly to her." Hosea 2:14.

Be EXCITED when your husband calls or comes by. Keep praise music going so you are always uplifted. It's not pursuing to be excited, it's alluring. Let him know by your excitement, enthusiasm and the tone of your voice that he is special and very loved by you. However, if you have never let him go, it will drive him away. You must FIRST be sure he KNOWS that you have truly let him go, then begin to allure him with your kind words. (For more on alluring get our Q&A video "Alluring and Unconditional Love.")

By agreement. Many ask what they should do if their unfaithful husbands approach them for physical intimacy. "But because of immoralities, let each man have his own wife, and let each woman have her own husband. Let the husband fulfill his duty to his wife, and likewise also the wife to her husband. The wife does not have authority over her own body, but the husband does; and likewise also the husband does not have authority over his own body, but the wife does. Stop depriving one another, *except by* **agreement** *for a time that you may devote yourselves to prayer*, and come together again lest Satan tempt you because of your lack of self-control." 1Cor. 7:2-5.

If you are still legally married, yet you refuse to be intimate, resist his advances, order him out of your bed or initiate sleeping apart (for whatever reason), you are working and playing into the hands of the devil. A woman who is an unbeliever would certainly order her husband out of her bed or out of her house. "And if you love those who love you, what credit is that to you? For even sinners love those who love them." Luke 6:32.

When a sinner or anyone who was "unclean" came to Jesus, He always responded kindly and even touched them. He says that anyone who comes to Him, He will in no way cast out! (John 6:37) No matter how often a sinner comes to the Lord, He always accepts him back even though He knows that he will soon reject Him again. Are you an imitator of Christ?

However, the above verse clearly covers those who are still legally married. If a divorce has taken place, give no appearance of evil. This is the time that you must abstain from intimacy at your former husband's request.

Personal commitment: to forgive. "Based on what I have learned in Scripture, I commit to trusting the Lord and refusing to fight in the flesh. I will continue daily to forgive my husband and all who have been involved. I will stay gentle and quiet as I walk in a spirit of forgiveness."

Date: _____ Signed:_____

Chapter

15

Comfort Those

*"Comfort those who are in **any** affliction
with the comfort with which we ourselves
are comforted by God."*
2Corinthians 1:4

Let me begin by assuring you that basically ALL the principles in this book will help to restore your marriage whether your husband is abusive or has a drinking, drug, or pornography problem. Most of the women who come to our ministry are dealing with adultery and one or more of the sins mentioned above.

When women come to us, they want to know: "How can I deal with and overcome the destruction that has plagued our lives for YEARS? How can I possibly make it through this pain and this mess?" The answer is, by seeking wisdom and truth. Prov. 23:23 says, "Buy truth, and do not sell it, get wisdom and instruction and understanding." My heart's desire is to share the truth with you in order to set you free. "...and you shall know the truth, and the truth shall make you free." John 8:32.

Dealing with Your Husband's Sins

If your husband is in any sin, how should you, as his wife, deal with it? Not as the world does!! The world's ways will bring about destruction, but God's principles will bring victory. Here is God's prescription, straight from His Word:

Without a Word. As we learned earlier, the Bible is clear that we are to reverently keep quiet and not try to talk to our husbands when they are disobedient to God's Word (1Pet. 3:1-2). Do not make the mistake of talking to your husband about his sin; talk to God only. Also, I would urge you not to talk to others about it either. Two things happen when you do. First, it puts us at odds with the Lord. "Whoever secretly slanders his neighbor, him I [God] will destroy..." Ps. 101:5.

Secondly, when you uncover his sins and weaknesses to others it makes it almost impossible for him to come back and repent. When everyone in the church, and all of your family and friends know that he has been living in adultery (or some other sin) you have made it almost impossible for him to come back. We are not to confess someone else's sins. Confessing your own sins is very different from revealing someone else's. It also brings about its own curse. "...Ham, the father of Canaan, saw the nakedness of his father, and **told** his two brothers outside....So he said, Cursed be Canaan." Gen. 9:22-25.

This verse confirms the principle that we read earlier in Prov. 101:5. We are told not to slander anyone! Nevertheless, I am keenly aware that it is very difficult to keep all that you are going through a secret. That is why we are told in Matt. 6:6 to "...go into your inner room, and when you have shut your door, pray to your Father who is in secret, and your Father who sees in secret will repay you." When you have no one to talk to, you *have to* pour your heart out to God! He is the only One who can really change your husband and your situation anyway! But when we tell everyone who asks or will listen, when we talk on the phone for hours about it, or even pour it all out to our pastor or counselor, we will fail to use that urgency in our prayer closet! I encourage women to do what works. I know personally that this works, and any other solution does not.

Fast. The greatest way to free a husband who is in bondage to sin is to fast and pray for him. "Is this not the fast which I choose, to loosen the bonds of wickedness, to undo the bands of the yoke, and to let the oppressed go free, **and break EVERY yoke?**" Isa. 58:6. There is more on fasting in Chapter 16, "Keys of Heaven" that you need to read.

Overcome evil with good! The other way is to overcome the evil by doing good! "Do not be overcome by evil, but overcome evil with good." Rom. 12:21. The Bible does not lie. Though the "experts" of today tell you that you "enable" the person who drinks, takes drugs, etc. by being kind and loving, Scripture tells us the opposite. Which will you choose to believe and obey? Love is one of the most powerful weapons we have and it is guaranteed to work. The Lord tells us that it is how we are to deal with our enemies or those who hurt us. Loving your husband right now, right in the midst of his sin, is truly overcoming evil with good!

Prov. 10:12 "...**love** covers **all** transgressions.

1Pet. 4:8 "Above all, keep **fervent in your love** for one another, because **love** *covers* **a multitude of sins**.

1Cor. 13:8 "Love **never** fails..."

1Thes. 5:15 "See that no one repays another with evil for evil, but always seek after that which is good **for one another** and for all men."

Rom. 12:14 "Bless those who *persecute* you; **bless and curse not**. Rejoice with those who rejoice, and weep with those who weep. Be of the same mind toward one another; do not be haughty in mind, but associate with the lowly. Do not be wise in your own estimation. **Never pay back evil for evil to anyone**. Respect what is right in the sight of all men."

Jesus said these words in Matt. 5:44-46: "But I say to you, **love your enemies,** and pray for those who persecute you...For if you love those who love you, what reward have you? Do not even the tax-gatherers [or sinners] do the same?"

Testimony: She Told Her Husband to Get Out!

A woman came to Restore Ministries who was angry, resentful and bitter! She had searched everywhere for help - support groups, counselors, and many books - in order to solve the problems she was having with her husband who she said was an "alcoholic" and drug "addict."

She had had enough! She had thrown her husband out of the house – as she had done a couple of times before. She had been following everyone's advice; unfortunately, nothing seemed to change her situation but inevitably things got much worse. What she learned from our ministry was different from anything else she had read or heard before. Finally, she said, she heard the truth.

She said she finally learned that the reasons for her problems were altogether different than what she had been told repeatedly. She told us that she had been so totally indoctrinated in psychology and unbiblical ideas that she could no longer discern the truth. When she read the principles, the Word of God became a sword, cutting through to her very marrow!

She learned about the danger of ruling over her husband, as when she had told him to leave the house. She learned the right way to win a disobedient husband: without a word. She learned how to deal with a man who was bound to the sin of alcohol, to fast and pray for him. She learned that a forced separation encourages adultery and would ALWAYS exaggerate her trials.

Within one week, she looked up every Bible verse listed in this book and marked them in her Bible. To her astonishment, she could find NO Scriptural basis for the actions she had taken with her husband.

She even called her church and begged them to show her that what she had been doing was really correct. She said she needed to discredit those Scriptures she had read in this book. They could give her no scriptural support. They just encouraged her to keep her husband out of the home, and not allow him to return.

In all her confusion, pain and anger, this woman really was searching for the truth. She finally asked her husband to return home. Then she gave him respect as the head of the household and spiritual leader for the first time in their marriage. The rebuilding of their home was not easy nor quick, yet it was ALWAYS stable. Her husband later confessed that he had been planning to commit adultery after she had forced him to leave. Her husband has been home for over nine years, drug and alcohol free! He is even a deacon at a large church.

Testimony: Husband Delivered from Alcohol

A woman contacted our ministry. She had hit the bottom with her husband's drinking. She had tried applying every method that she read for wives of alcoholics. Yet, she found that every recovery was only temporary. Their marriage was falling apart.

They had become estranged. She felt that if he really loved her he would stop drinking. However, her husband was convinced that she no longer loved him because of the way she was treating him. He said her ill treatment only made him drink more because he felt things were hopeless. She told us that she did love her husband but all the books said to withdraw from him because they were codependent and she had become his "enabler." She told us that she had "tried everything" and was ready to give up. We encouraged her to "seek God." She said that she had tried that. She said that she had gone to her pastor who confronted her husband, but that only made things worse –- he left the church.

When she finally reached the end of herself, she cried out to the Lord. The next morning she met a woman who had a restored marriage and who agreed to pray for her. Just two weeks later, when she thought her husband was at work, she got a phone call from him. He was at Teen Challenge seeking help. This woman's husband came out, three months later, a totally new man on fire for the Lord. He became the spiritual leader of their family and active in their new church. *You can try everything, but when you do, I promise, you only make matters worse. Try God ALONE!! Go after God, trust Him and He will change your situation in an instant.*

Do Not Provoke Them

Scripture warns us, "...do not harass them nor provoke them..." Deut. 2:19. When you provoke someone who is under the influence of drugs, alcohol or the seductions of an adulterous woman, you put yourself in grave danger. Prov. 18:6 tells us,"A fool's lips bring strife, and his mouth calls for blows."

If physical violence has become a part of your marriage, you need to heed this Bible verse and make sure that it is not occurring because of your disrespectful attitude and words toward your husband. God warns women not to even speak to a husband who is being disobedient to the Word and to make sure we are silent with a respectful attitude (see 1Pet. 3:1-2). God also tells us in Eph. 5:33 that "the wife (should) see to it that she respect her husband."

So often, after you verbally attack your husband's character, someone takes a swing. Often it is the woman who hits first because she is so hurt by something her husband has said. Unfortunately, after the first punch, physical violence becomes the norm. And once violence is brought into a home or a marriage, it becomes a major part of the destruction.

Testimony: In Her Own Words

I read this testimony in Crowned With Silver magazine. I am reprinting it for you, with permission from CWS and the writer of the article.

The following story is, I hope, an encouragement to others who may be in the situation in which I found myself. God has many ways of reaching people and my story is one which may cause the hardened of heart to call me "Raca," or "fool," but the Lord reached my husband through some very difficult circumstances. I ask, dear sisters, that you don't place my name at the end of the article, for I am concerned that my husband would not receive the honor that is due him in the eyes of my children if they read this.

My husband and I grew up in a community church and married as high school sweethearts. I was always a stay-at-home mother, and my husband was an automobile mechanic. We were from very different types of families. He grew up with four brothers and two sisters; I came from a family with just two girls. His family members were always loudly arguing, debating, and throwing a punch here and there when they were making a point. My family was very quiet. When my sister and I argued, we did it silently and maliciously. We wouldn't use words to get back at one another; we would do something to get even.

At the beginning of our marriage we were baby Christians, but I had a thirsting for more of God. My husband was content right where he had been for 23 years. He had made a confession of faith, and knew he was heaven bound. That was good enough for him. I, on the other hand, knew there had to be more. I knew that God was enough to sustain me throughout the rest of my life and I wanted to live a life different from the world around me.

We struggled financially. With the birth of our first daughter we were barely making it in our one-room apartment. My husband was like a tightrope. I'd try to keep the baby quiet in order to make life more peaceful and less irritating to him. Our relationship was better during the weekdays because he wasn't home that much. But we fought on the weekends. And then I would start my old tactics that I'd used growing up on my sister.

I wouldn't fight back, or yell, or scream. I would simply... get even. When we were arguing, I wouldn't make dinner, or I wouldn't do the laundry for a week and he would have to wear dirty clothing. I'd do something that I knew would get under his skin. But it wouldn't be something that he could actually point his finger at me for. I could get away with it because it wasn't blatant. Life went on like this for some years. We had the two girls back then, and then that tightrope that my husband and I were walking on snapped.

One Saturday, we were arguing about how we should spend the extra $20 out of the paycheck. My husband wanted to go to the ball game; I wanted him to take us out to dinner. He yelled that he worked for the money and he deserved a little time out for fun, and he turned to leave. So I gave him a little ... shove with my elbow. (I think all the built-up pressures from all the arguing and strife that was constant in our life somehow brought back his interaction with his brothers.) He immediately lifted his arm and socked me back in my arm as hard as he could. Never had I seen so much fury directed at someone - me!

The pain of it. I think that it wasn't the physical pain so much as the emotional and spiritual pain. See, I had been trying to grow in the Lord in all areas but my marriage. It was a torture to read the Scriptures which talk about how the Lord is the bridegroom and we are the bride, and somehow our marriage was supposed to be an example of our relationship with Christ. That was horrifying!

If my marriage and the relationship I had with my husband was in any way related to my relationship with Christ I was in big trouble! I think that once the restraint was gone, the taboo of hitting your spouse having been broken, my husband felt hopeless. More and more fighting would break out like this. I would try to hide it from the children, but sometimes there was no way to do this. I think this hurt me more than anything else.

Proverbs tells us that children's fathers are their glory. If fathers were supposed to be their glory, then my children must have felt betrayed and distrustful of all things, even God. As they were being taught the Scriptures, they were going to come to distrust even them if something didn't happen to heal this broken marriage.

And yes, even though my husband and I were married and not divorced, we had a broken marriage. I never told any of my friends at church what I was going through. I did tell one of my closest friends that my "cousin" had been going through certain things in order to get some advice, or to talk through the issues. But all the advice this friend gave me was that I should leave the monster. She said that there were names for this type of treatment and that only a fool would stay with such a man.

But there was one problem. It was a vow I had made to God a few years back that I would stay with this man through sickness and in health, through the good and the bad, until death do us part.... And even though I felt that there was absolutely no love left in my being for the man I was married to, I still loved God. I loved God with every fiber of my being. I loved Him so much that I would not break my marriage vows which I had said before Him those seven years ago.

Staying with my husband was a commitment I had made to the Lord the day that we were married before Him. I turned to our Heavenly Father. So many times in the past I had turned to secular advice in reading materials. I'd listen to my friends bad-mouth their husbands, and so on. I knew that the only way I was going to get any help at all was by seeking the Lord and finding Him and His help.

The Lord revealed Truth to me in some very simple ways. I needed to stop blaming my husband as the world tells us to do, and look at the things I was doing wrong in my marriage. Putting aside the hatred, anger, and resentment I felt for my spouse, I decided to replace those emotions with forgiveness, understanding and love. I repented of getting even in so many ways in order to make my husband miserable. And the Lord started changing me!

There is so much more to tell, but let me only say that God is in the changing business. If we yield our whole lives to Him, He is there to guide us through our darkest hours! I've now been married for 21 years to the same man. Well, he isn't the same man, as he gave his whole life to God as I did about 11 years ago. Just as he had felt the resentment and hate oozing from every pore of my being, so did he start feeling love and forgiveness flowing towards him.

Now we don't argue as we used to do, for both of us love each other so much that we want what the other person wants. We no longer put ourselves before the other's needs! God is wonderful! See, the Lord changed me first, and then He changed my husband! But it was the Lord who did the changing!

Testimony: Hide Me Under the Shadow of Your Wings

Elaine* had suffered so much abuse. From the time she was pregnant with her first child, her husband had repeatedly, in a rage, abused her. She had tried everything: shelters, friends' homes, going back home to her parents, even law enforcement officers, but nothing was permanent.

After her husband's violent explosions, he would become repentant, remorseful, even kind to her. He would seek to try and "make it up to her." He would plead with her to "please forgive" him. Being a Christian, she would. But all too soon, he would again become violent.

After three children and no hope in sight, she thought of taking her own life. But how could she leave her children with this violent man?

She couldn't. She would have to take their little lives as well. But murder! She had thought several times about killing her husband, especially in the
midst of his attacks. But how could she, a Christian, think like this?

One night she went to a prayer meeting at her church. There was no altar call, but Elaine walked slowly to the front of the church during the last song, and left her burdens there. For the first time that she could remember, she gave the entire situation to the Lord.

She heaved tears of pain at the foot of the cross. She gave it all to Him. And she surrendered, "Lord if you want me to stay with this man, I will. I will never try to run away again or to seek help. I accept this life you have given me. My children are yours. Do whatever you will with all of us."

Elaine went home relieved that things were finally settled in her heart. The next day while her children were at school and she and the baby were grocery shopping, God MOVED IN HER LIFE. Her husband left his job, came home and packed his things. Elaine's husband disappeared that day. That was 21 years ago.

Elaine is still legally married to a man she has not seen or heard from in over two decades. Her children are all grown and her youngest daughter has just married. She and all her children have a close relationship with the Lord. Elaine still lives hidden under the shadow of His wings (Ps. 17:8)

"And they **overcame** him because of the *blood of the Lamb* and because of the **word of their testimony**, and they did not love their life even to death." Rev. 12:11.

*Not her real name. **For many more powerful testimonies, visit our web page at www.RestoreMinistries.net or get the book** By the Word of Their Testimony *for encouragement.*

Personal commitment: to overcome evil with good. "Based on what I have learned in Scripture, I commit to renew my mind in God's truth. I will bless and pray for those who persecute me and overcome evil with good. I will trust the Lord and His protection rather than the arm of the flesh."

Date: _____ Signed:_____

16
The Keys of Heaven

*"I will give you the keys
of the kingdom of heaven...."
Matt. 16:19.*

Jesus gave us the keys of heaven to "bind up" the evil and "loose" the good. "I will give you the **keys** of the kingdom of **heaven**; and whatever you shall **bind** on earth shall be bound in heaven, and whatever you shall loose on earth shall be **loosed** in heaven." Matt. 16:19.

Remove the evil. Find a verse concerning what you want to remove. You must first bind the "strong man," which is the spirit that has a hold of the person you are praying for. Search for the verse that you can pray. "But *no one* can enter the strong man's house...unless he *first* **binds the strong man**...." Mark 3:27.

Replace the evil with good. This is very important! "When the unclean spirit goes out of a man, it passes through waterless places seeking rest, and not finding any, it says, '*I will return to my house from which I came.*' And when it comes, it finds it swept and put in order. Then it goes and takes along seven other spirits more evil than itself, and they go in and live there; and the last state of that man becomes **worse than the first**." Luke 11:24-26.

If you fail to replace. If you fail to replace what you have removed, it will become worse than before you prayed. You must always replace something evil with something good. This is one reason why so many who go on diets actually get fatter. Experts say that they stop eating all the bad, or try not to eat at all. But they never replace it with something good, like prayer, going for a walk, exercising, or eating something else that is good for them. Another example might be when someone has a very oily face. She scrubs it with soap and maybe puts alcohol on it to dry up the oil. Then after a few hours it's greasier than ever! Dermatologists will tell you that you must replace the oil you have removed with a small dab of lotion.

Replace the lies with the truth. The truth is only found in His Word. Unless what you hear, what you read, what someone tells you matches up with a principle in God's Word, IT IS A LIE!

Replace the "arm of the flesh" with the "Lord." Replace trusting in "the arm of the flesh" (you, a friend, whoever) with trusting in the Lord. "Finally, be strong in the Lord, and in the strength of His might." Eph. 6:10.

Replace running away with running to Him! "God is our refuge and our strength, a very present help in time of trouble." Ps. 46:1. Run to the book of Psalms! *Read Psalms (and Proverbs) every day. Read the Psalms that correspond to the day of the month plus 30 until the end, then read the corresponding Proverb (i.e. on the 5th of the month you would read Psalms 5, 35, 65, 95, 125 and Proverbs chapter 5.) An easy way to remember is to write where to turn on the bottom of the Psalm (i.e. on the bottom of the 6th Psalm you would write 36, on the bottom of 36 you would write 66. When you got to 126 you would write Prov. 6.) Since Psalm 119 is so long it is reserved for the 31st of the month.*

As a member of our Restoration Fellowship, you could go to our Daily Devotional on our website. Go to www.RestoreMinistries.net to join!

Replace crying out to another with crying out to Him! He promises to hear you and to lift you up immediately! But you **must** cry out! Don't think to yourself, "Well, God hasn't helped me in the past!" If He didn't help, it's simply because you didn't ask. "**Ask** *and it shall be given* you; seek and you shall find." Matt. 7:7.

Preparing for War

Put on your armor daily as described in Ephesians 6:10-18.

The schemes of the devil. "Finally, be strong in the Lord and in the strength of His might. Put on the full armor of God, that you may be able to stand firm against the schemes of the devil." Eph. 6:10-11. Remember who the real enemy is: Satan, not your husband.

The full armor of God. "For our struggle is not against flesh and blood, but against the rulers, against the powers, against the world forces of this darkness, against the spiritual forces of wickedness in the heavenly places. Therefore, take up the full armor of God, that you may be able to resist in the evil day." Eph. 6:12-13. You must resist the **fear** that causes you to run away or give up; stand firm and, having done everything, continue to stand firm. Psalm 37 is good to pray if you are plagued with fear.

Stand firm. "Stand firm therefore, having girded your loins with truth...." Eph. 6:14. People talk about "stepping out in faith." It may be best to stop moving and just stand firm! It may be the difference between trusting and tempting God. Sometimes we feel like we are taking a "step of faith," but we are actually throwing ourselves off a cliff, as Satan told Jesus to do.

Many times we should not be taking a "step" of faith but rather a "stand" in faith. Our convictions should enable us to "stand" for what is right. If we move, we could be falling off a cliff. If God brings adversity into our lives, our **stand** will be the testimony. Yet, as you will see later in this lesson, sometimes we are asked to step out and walk on water, as Peter was asked to do. Discernment is needed here. One rule that may help is the amount of urgency. Usually our "flesh" brings about urgency; God usually says to wait.

His righteousness. "...and having put on the breastplate of righteousness...." Eph. 6:14. God is talking about His righteousness, not yours. He tells us in His Word that our righteousness is nothing but "filthy rags" (Isa. 64:6).

Walk in peace. "And having shod your feet with the preparation of the gospel of peace..." Eph. 6:15. You can claim the promise in Matthew: "Blessed are the peacemakers!" Be peaceful with EVERYONE at ALL times!

The shield of faith. "In addition to all, taking up the shield of faith with which you will be able to *extinguish all the flaming missiles* of the evil one." Eph. 6:16. You must have faith – not in yourself or someone else like a shelter or a judge – faith in God, in Him alone! Circumstance has nothing to do with faith. Believe His Word alone for the truth about your situation.

Helmet of salvation. "And take the helmet of salvation."

Eph. 6:17. You must be saved; you must be one of His children to really win a difficult spiritual battle. It's as easy as talking to God right now. Just tell Him in your own words that you need Him, now. Ask Him to make Himself real to you. Give Him your life, a life that is messed up, and ask the Lord to make it new.

Tell Him that you will do whatever He asks, since He is now your Lord. Ask Him to "save you" from your situation and from the eternity that is waiting for all those who do not accept His gift of eternal life. Thank Him for His death on the cross, the death that He died for you. You can now believe that you will no longer live alone; God will always be with you and you will spend eternity in Heaven.

Sword of the Spirit. "Take...the sword of the Spirit which is the word of God." Eph. 6:17. This is exactly what we have been teaching: use His Word for a battle that will be won. When the battle is the Lord's, the victory is ours! Write down on 3x5 cards the Scriptures you need to help in your battle. Keep them with you at all times in your purse. When you feel an attack coming on, like fear, read the verses that pertain to fear. (See Rom. 8:15 and Psalm 23 for wonderful verses to attack fear.) Cry out to God. Stand firm in faith. "Be still and know that I am God." Ps. 46:10.

Pray at all times. "With all prayer and petition pray at all times in the Spirit." Eph. 6:18. Pray from deep in your Spirit. Have designated times of prayer three times a day (as Daniel did). That was one of the reasons he was thrown into the lions' den. Don't worry, but remember that even if you are in essence thrown into the lions' den, God will shut all the lions' mouths!

Be on the alert. "And with this in view, be on the alert with all perseverance and petition for all the saints." Eph. 6:18. Pray for another person you know each time fear overwhelms you. "Most gladly therefore, I will rather boast about my weaknesses, that the power of Christ may dwell in me. Therefore I am well content with weaknesses, with insults, with distresses, with persecutions, with difficulties, for Christ's sake; for when I am weak, then I am strong." Phil 12:9-10. After you have prayed for someone, call them and tell them.

Pray for those who persecute you. God also asked that we pray for someone else: our enemies, every one of them. Pray for them and ask God to show you what He wants you to do to bless them. It wasn't until after Job prayed for his so-called friends that God restored what Job had lost. "And the Lord restored the fortunes of

Job when he prayed for his friends, and the Lord increased all that Job had twofold." Job 42:10. "But I say to you, love your enemies, and pray for those who persecute you." He goes on to tell you why: "in order that you may be sons of your Father who is in heaven." Matt. 5:44-45.

Know God's Word

His Word will not come back void. You must know and learn God's Word. You need to set out to find the blessed promises of God. These principles are from His Word and when we speak His Word to Him by prayer, it will not come back void.

That is His promise to you! "So shall My word be which goes forth from My mouth; *it shall not return to Me void* (empty), without **accomplishing** what I desire and without **succeeding** in the matter for which I sent it." Isaiah 55:11. His desire was that you may overcome the evils in this world. You must do what is guaranteed by God Himself. Accept no imitations or counterfeits.

Search for His principles throughout your Bible. Seek understanding. God says if you seek you will find. God's Word gives wisdom. Looking deeper into the meaning gives you a better understanding. "And I say to you, ask, and it shall be given to you; **seek**, and **you shall find**; knock, and it shall be opened to you." Luke 11:9. And once you know what to do, then you can apply it to your life. "By **wisdom** a house is *built*, and by **understanding** it is *established*; and by **knowledge** the *rooms are filled* with all *precious* and *pleasant riches*." Prov. 24:3-4.

Read His Word with delight. Mark the verses in your Bible. "**Delight** yourself in the Lord; and He will give you the desires of your heart." Ps. 37:4. Take the time to mark verses for quick reference in times of distress (or when leading another to the truth). In Luke 4:4-10 what did Jesus answer when Satan was trying to tempt Him? "And Jesus answered him, 'It is written..., It is written..., for it is written....'" *Use a yellow crayon or specific light colors for different promises.*

Memorize. Meditate day and night. Memorize the promises you find so that the blessed assurance of them may sink into your soul. You must learn and know God's promises if you ever want to depend on Him alone. "But his delight is in the law of the Lord, And in His law he **meditates day and night**. And he will be like a tree firmly planted by streams of water, which yields its fruit in its season, And its leaf does not wither; And in whatever he does, he prospers." Ps. 1:2.

No matter how bad things seem, God is in control. Our comfort is knowing that God is in control, not us and certainly not Satan. "Simon, Simon, behold, Satan has **demanded** *permission* to sift you like wheat; but I have prayed for you, that your faith may not fail; and you, when *once you have turned again*, strengthen your brothers." Luke 22:31-32.

Sifting. Jesus knew the outcome, yet Peter still had to go through the "sifting" to be ready for God's calling on his life. Will you be ready when He calls you? "And let endurance have its perfect result, that you may be **perfect and complete**, *lacking in nothing.*" Jas. 1:4.

Spiritual Warfare

Take your thoughts captive. Your battle WILL be won or lost in your mind. "We are **destroying speculations** and every lofty thing raised up against the knowledge of God, and we are **taking every thought captive** to the obedience of Christ, and we are ready to punish all disobedience, whenever your obedience is complete." 2Cor. 10:5-6. Don't play into the enemies' hands. Don't entertain evil thoughts. Take them captive!

The Power of Three

Two or three gathered together. Find two other WOMEN who will pray with you. "But Moses' hands were heavy. Then they took a stone and put it under him, and he sat on it; and Aaron and Hur supported his hands, one on one side and one on the other. Thus his hands were steady until the sunset...when Moses held his hand up, then Israel prevailed, and when he let his hand down Amalek (the enemy) prevailed." Ex. 17:11-12.

Find **two** other **women** to hold you up so you won't become too weary. Pray and ask God to help you find two others who are like-minded. You can find an Encouragement Partner on our website.

The power of three. "And if **one** can *overpower him* who is alone, **two** can *resist* him. A cord of **three** strands is not quickly *torn apart.*" Eccl. 4:12.

To lift the other up. "**Two** are *better* than **one** because they have a *good return for their labor*. For if either of them *falls*, the *one will* *lift up his companion.* But woe to the one who falls when there is not another to lift him up." Eccl. 4:9-10.

He is there with you. "For where **two or three** have *gathered* together in My name, there I am in their midst." Matt. 18:20. "Then Nebuchadnezzar the king was astounded and stood up in haste; he responded and said to his high officials, 'Was it not **three men** we cast bound into the midst of the fire?' They answered and said to the king, 'Certainly, O king.' He answered and said, 'Look! I see **four men** loosed and walking about in the midst of the fire without harm, and the appearance of the **fourth** is like a *son of the gods!*' " Dan. 3:24. You are never alone!

Agreement. "Again I say to you, that if **two** of you *agree* on earth about **anything** that they may ask, it shall be done for them by My Father who is in heaven." Matt. 18:19. When you are wrestling with peace about something, call someone who is believing with you and pray in agreement.

Standing in the gap. "And I searched for a man among them who should build up the wall and **stand in the gap** before Me for the land, that I should not destroy it; but I *found no one.*" Ezek. 22:30.

Pray for one another. "Therefore, confess your sins to one another, and *pray for one another*, so that you may be healed. The effective prayer of a righteous man can accomplish much." Jas. 5:16. Also, confession to a like-minded woman is the best way to obtain a pure heart.

Make your confession. Ezra knew what to do when praying: "Now while Ezra was praying and **making confession**, weeping and prostrating himself before the house of God...." Ezra 10:1. Keep confessing the truth.

When do you give up praying? Never! We have a wonderful example of the fact that God does not always mean no when we don't have answered prayer.

Your faith is great. The Canaanite woman continued to beg Jesus for her daughter's healing. The result: "...Then Jesus answered and said to her, 'O woman, **your faith is great**; be it done for you as you wish.' And her daughter was healed at once." Matt. 15:2. When we pray for something that is clearly in God's will and it seems to have gone unheard or He has said what we think is "No," God may simply mean for us to keep on asking, waiting, pleading, fasting, believing, weeping, laying ourselves prostate before Him!

The battle for his soul. Are you unequally yoked? The real battle in your home is the battle for your husband's soul! Are you unequally yoked? Remember that you have the promise: "...you will be saved, you and all your household." Acts 11:14. Remember, **a husband is sanctified through his wife.** "For the unbelieving husband is *sanctified through his wife*...For how do you know, O wife, whether you will save your husband?" 1Cor. 7:14-17.

Prayer and Fasting

Prayer AND fasting. Jesus told His apostles, "But this kind does not go out *except* by **prayer and fasting.**" Matt. 17:21. If you have been praying fervently and have checked to see if your ways are pure, then fasting may be called for. There are different lengths of fasts:

Three-day fast. Esther fasted "for favor" from her husband the king. She fasted 3 days "for favor." "Go, assemble all the Jews who are found in Susa, and **fast** for me; do not eat or drink for *three days*, night or day. I and my maidens also will **fast** in the same way." Esth. 4:16. This fast (or the 7-day) has another benefit for those who are contentious or who can never stop talking. You will become too weak to argue!!

Day fast. The day fast begins in the evening after your evening meal. You drink only water until the 24-hour period is complete, then eat the next day's evening meal. You fast and pray during this time for your petition. This fast can be done a couple of times a week.

Seven-day fast. There is a fast that is 7 days (seven days seems to represent completion). "Now it came about when I heard these words, I sat down and wept and mourned **for days**; and **I was fasting and praying** before the God of heaven." Neh. 1:4. Usually it will be during great sorrow that you are "called" to fast for seven days.

My knees are weak from fasting. When you are hungry or weak, use that time for prayer and reading His Word. "**My knees are weak from fasting**; and my flesh has grown lean, without fatness." Ps. 109:24.

In order to be seen. Keep as quiet about your fast as is possible. During the fast, you are to be silent, never complaining or drawing attention to yourself. "And whenever you **fast**, do not put on a **gloomy face** as the *hypocrites* do, for they neglect their appearance **in order to be seen** fasting by men. Truly I say to you, they have their *reward in full*. But you, when you fast, anoint your head, and wash your face so *that you may not be seen fasting by men*, but by your Father who is in secret; and *your Father who sees in secret will repay you.*" Matt. 6:16-18.

Many write me because they say they can't fast. If it is for medical reasons or pregnancy, then fast "any good thing." If, however, you think you can't fast because you are working – you are selling yourself and God short!

When the battle has been won, stand and see. Once you know that you have prayed, as we have been reading throughout Scripture, then do as it says: "You need not *fight* in this **battle**; station yourselves, *stand and see* the salvation of the Lord on your behalf." 2Chron. 20:17.

No one should boast. God says we are a stubborn people. When a battle is won or when the war is over, let us only boast in Him. Let us remain humble. "For by grace you have been saved through faith; and that not of yourselves, it is the **gift of God**; not as a result of works, that *no one should boast.*" Eph. 2:8-9.

"Do not say in your heart... 'Because of **my righteousness** the Lord has brought me in to possess this land,' but because of the wickedness...that the Lord is dispossessing them before you. It is not for your righteousness or for the **uprightness of your heart** that you are going to possess their land, but *because* of *the wickedness* of these...for you are a **stubborn people**...you have been rebellious against the Lord." Deut. 9:4-7.

We all have sinned and come short of the glory of God. So let us remember this when the battle is won. Our righteousness is nothing but filthy rags. Glory in Him!

Intensity of your trials is a sign that you are close to victory. Your trials may intensify when you are close to gaining the victory. "For this reason, **rejoice**, O heavens and you who dwell in them. Woe to the earth and the sea, because the devil has come down to you, having great wrath, *knowing* that he has only a **short time**." Rev. 12:12.

You must battle in the proper way. Do what God says; it *will* work! Don't try to defend yourself; it creates war and hard hearts. "To sum up, let all be harmonious, sympathetic, brotherly, kindhearted, and humble in spirit; not returning *evil for evil*, or *insult for insult*, but **giving a blessing instead**; for you were called for the very purpose that you might **inherit a blessing**." 1Pet. 3:8. Make sure you go the extra mile and bless your husband. Ask God how He wants you to bless him.

This is a spiritual battle. "Do you think that I cannot appeal to My Father, and He will *at once* put at My disposal more than twelve legions of angels." Matt. 26:52. Our heavenly Father will call on the angels to battle for your behalf in the "heavenlies" where the "real battle" is waging. "For our struggle is **not against flesh and blood**, but against the rulers, against the powers, against the world forces of wickedness **in the heavenly places**." Eph. 6:12.

Your husband is not the enemy. "Do you not know when you present yourselves to someone as slaves of obedience, you are slaves of the one whom you obey, either of sin resulting in death, or of obedience resulting in righteousness?" Rom. 6:16. A person in sin is really just a slave of the devil.

We may think the one who sins is awful, but so are we, if we continue to react with vengeance. (Remember, that belongs to Him alone!) "For though we walk in the flesh, we do not war according to the flesh, for the **weapons of our warfare** are not of the flesh, but **divinely powerful** for the *destruction of fortresses*." 2Cor. 10:4. Let's get at the root cause rather than just the symptom.

Be committed. Be committed regardless of the consequences and leave the results to God. "If it be so, our God whom we serve is able to deliver us from the furnace of blazing fire; and He will deliver us out of your hand, O king. But even if He does not, let it be known to you, O king, that we are not going to serve your gods or worship the golden image that you have set up." Dan. 3:17.

These boys believed that God would deliver them, but regardless of the consequences they were resolved to obey the Lord anyway. Even if they should die in the furnace, they would do what they knew God wanted them to do and they left the results with God. The boys didn't die, but the cords that bound them were removed through their walking in the fire. Do you have cords (of sin or worry) that are binding you? God will deliver. **It's His battle! Call on the God of Hosts; He is the warrior.**

To post a prayer request or to find an Encouragement Partner who will faithfully pray for you, your needs and be there for you when a crisis hits, go to our website at: www.RestoreMinistries.net.

Chapter

17

Stand in the Gap

*"And I searched for a man among them
who should build up the wall and
stand in the gap before Me
for the land, that I should not destroy it;
but I found no one."
Ezekiel 22:30*

"Dear Heavenly Father, I enter into my prayer closet and, now that I have shut the door, I pray to you my Father in secret. And as you see me here in secret you will reward me openly. It is written that all things, whatsoever ye shall ask in prayer, believing, ye shall receive.

"O God, thou art my God; early will I seek thee; my soul longs for Thee in a dry and thirsty land,where no water is. Lord, there is no one besides Thee to help in the battle between the powerful and those who have no strength; so help us, O Lord our God, for we trust in Thee, and in Thy name have come against this multitude. O Lord, Thou art my God; let not man prevail against Thee.

"Your eyes, Lord, move to and fro throughout the whole earth that you may strongly support those hearts who are completely Yours. Search my heart.

"For though we walk in the flesh, we do not war after the flesh, for the weapons of our warfare are not carnal, but mighty through God to the pulling down of strongholds. Casting down imaginations, and every high thing that exalts itself against the knowledge of God, and bringing into captivity every thought to the obedience of Christ, and You have readiness to revenge all disobedience when Your obedience is fulfilled.

"O let the evil of the wicked come to an end, but establish the righteous. I shall not be afraid of evil tidings; my heart is fixed, trusting in the Lord. My heart is established; I shall not be afraid, until I see my desire come upon the enemy.

"Let my husband's fountain be blessed and let him rejoice with the wife of his youth. Let me, dear Lord, be as the loving hind and pleasant doe; let me have the hidden imperishable quality in my heart of a gentle and quiet spirit which is precious in your sight. For the ways of a man are before the eyes of the Lord and He watches all his paths.

"Whatsoever ye shall bind on earth shall be bound in heaven; and whatsoever ye shall loose on earth shall be loosed in heaven. I ask you, Heavenly Father, to rebuke and to bind Satan in the name and through the blood of my Lord Jesus Christ. Hedge up his way with thorns, and build a wall against him so that he cannot find his paths. Then you will say to me, dear Lord, 'Go again, love a man who is loved by his wife.' Therefore I will speak kindly to him. A man shall leave his father and mother and cleave to his wife and the two shall be one flesh.

"Abraham hoped against hope, believed in hope, and being not weak in faith, staggered not at the promise of God through unbelief; but was strong in faith, giving glory to God. He was fully persuaded that what He had promised, He was able to perform.

"For we are saved by hope; but hope that is seen is not hope; for what man seeth, why doth he yet hope for it? But if we hope for what we see not, then do we with patience wait for it. I had fainted, unless I had believed to see the goodness of the Lord in the land of the living. Wait on the Lord; be of good courage and He will strengthen thine heart, yes, wait on the Lord. But they that wait upon the Lord shall renew their strength; they shall mount up with wings as eagles; they shall run and not be weary; and they shall walk and not faint.

"For since the beginning of the world men have not heard, nor perceived by the ear, neither hath the eye seen, O God, beside thee, what He hath prepared for him who waiteth for Him. Surely goodness and mercy shall follow me all the days of my life and I will dwell in the house of the Lord forever. Amen."

Prayer for Those in Adultery

"I ask you, Father, to rebuke and bind Satan in the Name and through the Blood of the Lord Jesus Christ. I ask you to build a Hedge of Thorns around my husband so that anyone who is interested in him will lose interest and leave. I base my prayer on the command of Your Word which says, 'What therefore God has joined together, let no man separate.' I thank you, Father, for hearing and answering my prayer. Amen."

"Therefore I will hedge up his way with thorns, and I will build a wall against him so that he cannot find his paths. And he will pursue his lovers, but will not overtake them; and he will seek them, but will not find them. Then he will say, 'I will go back to my wife. For it was better for me then than now!' Therefore I will allure him, bring him into the wilderness, and speak kindly to him. For I will remove the names of Baals from his mouth. Then the Lord said to me, 'Go again, love a (man) yet an adulterer.' " *From Hosea 6.*

"Drink water from your own cistern, and fresh water from your own well. Should your springs be dispersed abroad, streams of water in the streets? Let them be yours alone, and not for strangers with you. Let your fountains be blessed, and rejoice in the wife of your youth. As a loving hind and graceful doe, let her breasts satisfy you at all times. For why should you, my son, be exhilarated with an adulteress, and embrace the bosom of a foreigner? Can man take fire to his bosom, and his clothes not be burned? Or can a man walk on hot coals, and his feet not be scorched? So is one who goes in to his neighbor's wife. Whoever touches her will not go unpunished. For the ways of a man are before the eyes of the Lord, and He watches all his paths." *From Proverbs 5.*

"Keep your way far from her, and do not go near to the door of her house, lest you give your vigor to others, lest strangers be filled with your strength, and your hard-earned goods go to the house of an alien; and you groan at your latter end. For on account of a harlot one is reduced to a loaf of bread, and an adulteress hunts for the precious life. He who keeps company with harlots wastes his wealth." *From Proverbs 5.*

"Do not let your heart turn aside to her ways, for the heart is like channels of water in the hand of the Lord; He turns it wherever He wishes. Do not stray into her paths. For many are the victims she has cast down, and numerous are all her slain. Her house is the way to Sheol, descending to the chambers of death. The mouth of an adulteress is a deep pit; he who is cursed of the Lord will fall into it.

For a harlot is a deep pit, and an adulterous woman is a narrow well." *From Proverbs 7.*

"The one who commits adultery with a woman is lacking sense; he who would destroy himself does it. Surely she lurks as a robber, and increases the faithless among men. Like a bird that wanders from her nest, so is a man who wanders from his home." *From Proverbs 6, 27.*

"This is the way of an adulterous woman; she eats and wipes her mouth and says, 'I have done no wrong.' For the lips of an adulteress drip honey and smoother than oil is her speech; but in the end she is bitter as wormwood and sharp as a two-edged sword. Her feet go down to death, she does not ponder the path of life; her ways are unstable, she does not know it." *From Proverbs 5.*

"You adulteresses, do you not know that friendship with the world is hostility with God? Therefore, whoever wishes to be a friend of the world makes himself an enemy of God. And do not participate in the unfruitful deeds of darkness, for it is disgraceful even to speak of the things which are done by them in secret." *From James 4.*

"For though we walk in the flesh, we do not war according to the flesh, for the weapons of our warfare are not of the flesh, but divinely powerful for the destruction of fortresses. We are destroying every lofty thing raised up against the knowledge of God, and we are taking every thought captive to the obedience of Christ.

"For I now rejoice, not that you were made sorrowful, but that you were made sorrowful to the point of repentance; for you were made sorrowful according to the will of God, in order that you might not suffer loss in anything through us. For the sorrow that is according to the will of God produces a repentance without regret, leading to salvation; but the sorrow of the world produces death." *Taken from 2Cor. 10.*

"God gave us a ministry of reconciliation, namely, that God Himself was in Christ reconciling the world to Himself, not counting their trespasses against them, and He has committed to us the word of reconciliation. Therefore, we are ambassadors for Christ, as though God were entreating through us; we beg you on behalf of Christ, be reconciled to God." *Taken from 2Cor. 5.*

"For God has said, Behold, I will cast her down upon a bed of sickness, and those who commit adultery with her into great tribulation, unless they repent of her deeds. Therefore, confess your sins one to another, and pray for one another, so that you may be healed. The effectual prayer of a righteous man can accomplish much. For he who conceals his transgressions will not prosper, but he who confesses and forsakes them will find compassion." *Taken from Rev. 2:22.*

"There will be more joy in heaven over one sinner who repents, than over ninety-nine righteous persons who do not need repentance. Yes, there is joy in the presence of the angels of God over one sinner who repents. For Jesus said, 'He who is without sin among you, let him be the first to throw a stone. I do not condemn you; go your way. From now on sin no more.'" *Taken from Luke 15.*

"Neither do I condemn you." *John 8.*

Prayer to Restore

"Hear my prayer, O Lord, give ear to my cry, do not be silent at my tears. Put my tears in a bottle, are they not in Thy book? Since I am afflicted and needy, let the Lord be mindful of me. Thou art my help and my deliverer. Do not delay, O my God." *From Psalms 56 and 40.*

"My close friend in whom I trusted, who ate my bread, has lifted up his heel against me. For it is not an enemy who reproaches me, then I could bear it; nor is it one who hates me who has exalted himself against me, then I could hide myself from him. But it is you, a man my equal, my companion and my familiar friend, we who had sweet fellowship together." *From Psalms 41 and 55.*

"Let the evil of the wicked come to an end, but establish the righteous. In the net which they hid their own foot has been caught. Hold them guilty, O God, by their own devices, let them fall! In the multitude of their transgression thrust them out for they are rebellious against Thee. Let those be appalled because of their shame. All my enemies shall be ashamed and greatly dismayed. They shall turn back, they shall suddenly be ashamed. Let me not be put to shame, O Lord, for I call upon Thee. Let the wicked be put to shame, let them be silent. In thee, O Lord, I have taken refuge. In Thy righteousness deliver me." *From Psalms 7, 9, and 31.*

"Though they intend evil against Thee, and devise a plot, they will not succeed. When my enemies turn back they stumble and perish before Thee. Thou hast blotted out their name forever and ever. The very memory of them has perished. Yet a little while and the wicked man will be no more. And you will look carefully for his place and he will not be there. But the humble will inherit the land and will delight themselves in abundant prosperity." *From Psalm 21.*

"Thou dost surround the righteous with a shield. In peace I will both lie down and sleep. For Thou alone dost make me dwell in safety. Offer to God a sacrifice of thanksgiving, and call upon Me in the day of trouble. I shall rescue you, and you will honor Me." *From Psalm 4.*

"Be strong, and let your heart take courage, all you who hope in the Lord. Be their shepherd also and carry them forever. I would have despaired if I had not believed that I would see the goodness of the Lord, in the land of the living. Wait for the Lord; be strong and let your heart take courage. Yes, wait for the Lord." *From Psalm 27.*

" 'For your husband is your Maker, Whose name is the Lord of Hosts; for the Lord has called you, like a wife forsaken and grieved in spirit, even a wife of one's youth when she is rejected,' says your God." Isaiah 54:5-6.

May God Grant You Victory!

Personal commitment: to battle in the Spirit for my husband and my marriage. "Based on what I have learned from God's Word, I commit to battling in the Spirit rather than continuing to battle in the flesh. I recognize that when I battle in the flesh I am losing the spiritual battle. Therefore I commit to spending my energy, time and thought life in the spiritual battle for my marriage and family."

Date: _____ Signed:_____

For encouragement and to build your faith, you will find pages of testimonies posted on our website or order our book of restored marriages "By the Word of Their Testimony" on our website below.

If your marriage has been restored through this book or through our ministry, please write to us so that we can post it on our website and publish it in our book of testimonies. Let's give HIM the praise He so rightly deserves and let's tell the world what God has done in our lives to encourage others. "They overcame him because of the blood of the Lamb and because of the *word of their testimony....*" Revelation 12:11.

www.RestoreMinistries.net

Content Index

Scripture Index

About the Author

Erin Thiele has been blessed to be the mother of four boys, Dallas, Axel, Easton, and Cooper, and three girls, Tyler, Tara and Macy. Her stand for marriage was founded on the rock during her struggle to restore her own marriage. Erin's husband Dan had left her for another woman and eventually divorced her.

Restore Ministries was begun when Erin searched every denomination in her area but was unable to find the help or hope that she needed.

This book and the workbook *A Wise Woman Builds Her House: By a FOOL Who Tore Hers Down with Her Own Hands* were originally one large book she wrote as the Lord led her to prepare her home for her husband's return. Later, this restoration book was taken out of the workbook to help the many women the Lord sent to Erin who were in crisis.

Since Dan's return in 1991, Erin has written other books with her distinctive style of using the Scriptures to minister to the brokenhearted and the spiritual captives. "He sent **His Word** and healed them, and delivered them from their destructions."

This is another powerful testimony to God's promises and His faithfulness. "For as many as may be the promises of God, in Him they are **Yes**; wherefore also by Him is our **Amen** to the glory of God through us." 2Cor. 1:20.

To purchase Dan and Erin's entire testimony on audio tape, go to their website at www.RestoreMinistries.net or call their toll-free line at: 1.800.397.0800.

"**The Spirit of the Lord God is upon me**,
Because the **Lord** has *anointed me*
To bring **good news** to the *afflicted*;
He has sent me to **bind up** the *brokenhearted*,
To proclaim **liberty** to *captives*,
And **freedom** to *prisoners*;
To proclaim the favorable year of the Lord,
And the day of vengeance of our God;
To **comfort** all who **mourn**,
To grant those who mourn in Zion,
Giving them a **garland** instead of *ashes*,
The oil of **gladness** instead of *mourning*,
The **mantle of praise** instead of a *spirit of fainting*.
So they will be **called** *oaks of righteousness*,
The **planting** of the *Lord*,
that **HE MAY BE GLORIFIED**.
Then they will **rebuild** the ancient *ruins*,
They will **raise up** the *former devastations*,
And they will **repair** the *ruined cities*,
The **desolations** of *many generations*."
Isaiah 61:1-4

We now have many resources for women to help see you through to *restoration*. Come to our on-line store to see what books, audio and video tapes are available to help and encourage you.

We invite you to join our Restoration Fellowship, on-line, to receive help, prayer and an ePartner (someone who is like-minded and going through the same situation that you are facing that will pray for you, encourage you and keep you accountable).

If you need prayer, come and post a prayer request on our website so that people from around the world will fast and pray for your marriage. If God is moving in your life and marriage, come to our website and post a Praise Report.

**Restore Ministries
International**
POB 495
Hartville, MO 65667
OrderLine: 800.397.0800

Please visit us at:

www.RestoreMinistries.net

"Let Another Praise You" Prov. 27:2

"Thank You so much LORD . . . for giving all of us Erin and Dan to assist You in bringing families together after enduring such hard times. The praise goes to the LORD; many thanks and blessings to Restore Ministries and their family for the work they do to help deliver His word in ways that many can understand. My wife of seventeen years divorced me but she now has been home for three weeks after a year and a half of being divorced and 21 months apart!" C.B.

"Erin, I want to thank you for what you do to help marriages. I am so thankful that God has restored my marriage and as I continue to seek Him, I now think I know what you mean.... BE STILL AND KNOW THAT I AM GOD!! Just two days after my mother's funeral my marriage was restored!! I had cried out to God for help because when I had also gone to my pastor and asked what could I do and he too just looked sad and said it was up to my husband; "but by the Grace of God" I found Restore Ministries!!!" B.J.

"After reading Restore's website, I stopped nagging and asking my husband when he was coming home. What a difference it made from when I thought I had to "express my feelings" and "win the war" as I lost peace for eight years! My marriage is finally restored!!" M.W.

"Erin, I want to thank-you so much for being so honest with all of us. Thank you for allowing the Lord to change you, and for allowing Him to help you spread the truth. My husband is home! He arrived home almost one year to the day that the Lord allowed him to leave. I was contentious, controlling, angry, suspicious, hurt, bitter, had committed adultery, and was ready to kill myself when he left. Would you believe that now he keeps telling me how lucky he is to have married me and now wants to "show me off" to his friends and family?!!" M.P.

"Praise God! Thank You Jesus, and thank you Restore Ministries for the guidance to get myself in tune with God's will!! God can and will restore if we let Him! IF WE LET JESUS DO IT, HE WILL DO IT!! PRAISE GOD!! PRAISE GOD!! Our home is finally "home" again, and Restore Ministries helped me see that it's not what I think or what the world thinks, BUT WHAT GOD WANTS ME TO THINK AND DO! Don't listen to peoples' opinions; go to God! Do what the Lord says and it will work!" D.D.

"Praise God with every breath that He gives us. I thank God for this wonderful ministry that I found when I was at my lowest. Erin and Dan, you have been like John the Baptist to me, pointing me to the direction of God, my first love. My husband is home, PTL!! He is more affectionate, considerate and tells our family that we must put God first! I can't help but cry tears of joy when I think about how far God has brought me and to know that God loves me even with all my shortcomings. Who wouldn't serve a God like this? Just P.U.S.H. (Pray Until Something Happens)." K.T.

"I am convinced also, as Erin is, that "marriage crises" are not about the marriage, but are actually "spiritual crises" in disguise. For those of you out there who are wondering if you need to apply all the Biblical principles that Erin suggests: JUST DO IT! My husband has been home now for a little over one month, and has shared with me one story after another that confirms this wisdom of following God's way!!" K.B.

*"Erin, I thought my husband and I were happily married until this summer when he grew cold and distant. I did not understand or react well to this and it quickly escalated into him telling me he doesn't love me and never did and even once that he hated me. I was drowning in despair and wanted to save my marriage but could find no help. Erin is so right about counseling -- it only made things worse!! (And my minor is in psychology!) A Christian friend led me to your site, which was a miracle in itself the way that happened, and I immediately embraced God and the teachings. **I was saved through the prayer I found on your website.** I am praying a lot and in the Word every day and I can see so many changes in myself and that my husband is responding to them, slowly but surely. I did not see any of my own sins until this all happened. The scales were definitely lifted from my eyes."* M.B.

**If you or someone you know is in a seemingly hopeless situation,
the truth is "with God, nothing is impossible."**

www.RestoreMinistries.net

**OrderLine:
1.800.397-0800**

WHY NOT LET GOD

RESTORE YOUR MARRIAGE?

"Three months ago I found out my husband was cheating on me. A friend bought me this book and two months later my husband got saved and our marriage was restored!!! Praise God!!!" J.S.

"Using this book as a road map, I am no longer anxious and filled with fear. This book has really impacted my life!" C.W.

"As I read the encouraging words in this book it seemed as though God had written them just to me." D.F.

"I have read this book about six times. I will NEVER stop - it is so good!!" E.W.

Is everyone telling you that your marriage is hopeless? It's not! God is more than able to restore any marriage, especially YOURS! Why should YOU be another divorce statistic when God's Word holds both the Power and the Truth to change YOUR seemingly hopeless situation?

Erin Thiele wrote this book for YOU during her struggle to restore her marriage. Her husband had left her for another woman and eventually divorced her. In desperation she searched for help. All the "experts" tried to convince her that her marriage was hopeless – then she found the Mighty Counselor and His Word!

Through the application of God's principles, which Erin has documented in this book, her marriage was miraculously and completely restored! Join the many women who have applied the principles in this book for *victory* instead of defeat!

ISBN 1-931800-00-6

5 1299>

9 781931 800006

The Penitentes

of the Southwest